GENERALLY SPEAKING

Generally Speaking

By

G. K. Chesterton

New York

Dodd, Mead & Company

1929

203798
LF

PR
4453
C4G4

fk

PRINTED IN THE UNITED STATES OF AMERICA
BY THE VAIL-BALLOU PRESS, INC., BINGHAMTON, N. Y.

CONTENTS

CONTENTS

GENERALLY SPEAKING

I. ON DETECTIVE NOVELS

It is now some years since Miss Carolyn Wells, the American lady who has produced many of our most charming stories of murder and mystification, wrote to a magazine to complain of the unsatisfactory sort of review accorded to that sort of book; but not yet has the abuse been corrected. She said it is only too obvious that the task of reviewing detective stories is given to people who do not like detective stories. She says, and I think not unreasonably, that this is very unreasonable: a book of poems is not sent to a man who hates poetry; an ordinary novel is not reviewed by a rigid moralist who regards all novels as immoral. If mystery stories have any right to be reviewed at all, they have a right to be reviewed by the sort of person who understands why they were written. And the lady proceeds to say that, by this neglect, the nature of the technique really required in such a tale is never adequately discussed. I, for one, agree with her that it is a matter well worthy of discussion. There is no better reading, and in the true sense no more serious reading, than the few critical passages which great critics have devoted to this literary question; such as Edgar Allan Poe's disquisition on analysis at the beginning of the beautiful idyll about the murderous ape; or the studies of Andrew Lang on the problem of Edwin Drood; or the remarks of Stevenson on the police novel at the end of *The Wrecker*. Any such discussion, clearly conducted, will soon show that the rules of art are as much involved in this artistic form as in any other; and it is not any objection to such a form that people can enjoy it who cannot criticize it. The same is true of any good song or any sound romance. By a curious confusion, many modern critics have passed from the proposition that a masterpiece may be unpopular to the other proposition that unless it is unpopular it cannot be a masterpiece. It is as if one were to say that because a clever man may have an impediment in his speech, therefore a man cannot be clever unless he stammers. For all unpopularity is a sort of obscurity; and all obscurity is a defect of expression like a stammer. Anyhow, I am in this matter on the popular side; I am interested in all sorts of sensational fiction, good, bad and indifferent, and would willingly discuss it with a much less capable exponent of it than the author of *Vicky Van*. And if anyone likes to say that my tastes are vulgar and inartistic and illiterate, I can only say I am quite content to be as vulgar as Poe and as inartistic and illiterate as Andrew Lang.

Now, it is all the more curious that the technique of such tales is not discussed, because they are exactly the sort in which technique is nearly the whole of the trick. It is all the more odd that such writers have no critical guidance, because it is one of the few forms of art in which they could to some extent be guided. And it is all the more strange that nobody discusses the rules, because it is one of the rare cases in which some rules could be laid down. The very fact that the work is not of the highest order of creation makes it possible to treat it as a question of construction. But while people are willing to teach poets imagination, they seem to think it hopeless to help plotters in a matter of mere ingenuity. There are text-books instructing people in the manufacture of sonnets, as if the visions of bare ruined quires where late sweet birds sang, or of the ground-whirl of the perished leaves of hope, the wind of death's imperishable wing, were things to be explained like a conjuring trick. We have monographs expounding the art of the Short Story, as if the dripping horror of the *House of Usher* or the sunny irony of the *Treasure of Franchard* were recipes out of a cookery book. But in the case of the only kind of story to which the strict laws of logic are in some sense applicable, nobody seems to bother to apply them, or even to ask whether in this or in that case they are applied. Nobody writes the simple book which I expect every day to see on the bookstalls, called *How to Write a Detective Story*.

I myself have got no further than discovering how

not to write one. But even from my own failures I
have gained stray glimpses of what such a scheme of
warnings might be. Of one preliminary principle I
am pretty certain. The whole point of a sensational
story is that the secret should be simple. The whole
story exists for the moment of surprise; and it should
be a moment. It should not be something that it takes
twenty minutes to explain, and twenty-four hours to
learn by heart, for fear of forgetting it. The best way
of testing it is to make an imaginative picture in the
mind of some such dramatic moment. Imagine a dark
garden at twilight, and a terrible voice crying out in
the distance, and coming nearer and nearer along the
serpentine garden paths until the words become
dreadfully distinct; a cry coming from some sinister
yet familiar figure in the story, a stranger or a servant from whom we subconsciously expect some such
rending revelation. Now, it is clear that the cry which
breaks from him must be something short and simple
in itself, as, "The butler is his father," or "The Archdeacon is Bloody Bill," or "The Emperor has cut his
throat," or what not. But too many otherwise ingenious romancers seem to think it their duty to discover what is the most complicated and improbable
series of events that could be combined to produce a
certain result. The result may be logical, but it is not
sensational. The servant cannot rend the silence of

the twilight garden by shrieking aloud: "The throat of the Emperor was cut under the following circumstances: his Imperial Majesty was attempting to shave himself and went to sleep in the middle of it, fatigued with the cares of state; the Archdeacon was attempting at first in a Christian spirit to complete the shaving operation on the sleeping monarch, when he was suddenly tempted to a murderous act by the memory of the Disestablishment Bill, but repented after making a mere scratch and flung the razor on the floor; the faithful butler, hearing the commotion, rushed in and snatched up the weapon, but in the confusion of the moment cut the Emperor's throat instead of the Archdeacon's; so everything is satisfactory, and the young man and the girl can leave off suspecting each other of assassination and get married." Now, this explanation, however reasonable and complete, is not one that can be conveniently uttered as an exclamation or can sound suddenly in the twilight garden like the trump of doom. Anyone who will try the experiment of crying aloud the above paragraph in his own twilight garden will realize the difficulty here referred to. It is exactly one of those little technical experiments, illustrated with diagrams, with which our little text-book would abound.

Another truth to which our little text-book would at least tentatively incline is that the *roman policier* should be on the model of the short story rather than the novel. There are splendid exceptions: *The Moonstone* and one or two Gaborius are great works in this style; as are, in our own time, Mr. Bentley's *Trent's Last Case,* and Mr. Milne's *Red House Mystery.* But I think that the difficulties of a long detective novel are real difficulties, though very clever men can by various expedients get over them. The chief difficulty is that the detective story is, after all, a drama of masks and not of faces. It depends on men's false characters rather than their real characters. The author cannot tell us until the last chapter any of the most interesting things about the most interesting people. It is a masquerade ball in which everybody is disguised as somebody else, and there is no true personal interest until the clock strikes twelve. That is, as I have said, we cannot really get at the psychology and philosophy, the morals and the religion, of the thing until we have read the last chapter. Therefore, I think it is best of all when the first chapter is also the last chapter. The length of a short story is about the legitimate length for this particular drama of the mere misunderstanding of fact. When all is said and done, there have never been better detective stories than the old series of Sherlock Holmes; and though the name of that magnificent magician has been spread over the whole world, and is perhaps the one great popular legend made in the modern world, I do not think that Sir Arthur Conan Doyle has ever been thanked enough for them. As one of many millions, I offer my own mite of homage.

II. ON THE YOUNG IDEA

THERE are two modern malcontents who are very often confused together. There is the man who grumbles because the poor are educated and the man who grumbles because they are not. A doubt about education is identified with a denial of education, in the sense of a refusal or repudiation of it in the abstract; a thing that does exist, but exists in a totally different type of man. He is, in my opinion, a highly offensive and foolish sort of man. Years ago he used to go about bursting with indignation because somebody wanted poor children taught the piano. Why they should not be taught the letter F on the piano as much as in the spelling-book I never could understand. But we might lawfully conduct an inquiry into exactly how much good is actually done by their learning either one or the other. Suppose that literally the only result of teaching a child the piano were that he went on hammering one note with one finger for hours at a time, not only without any notion of a tune, but without any notion that one note is supposed to follow another. We should not complain of his having learnt to play, but of his not having learnt to play. We should recognize that a piano is in itself an ingenious and harmonious structure; but we should still think that a piano without a piano-player was something of a white elephant; and none the less for having, like any other white elephant, a magnificent display of ivory. Now that sort of result, in relation to the piano, would be something like the ultimate result in relation to the spelling-book. A spelling-book is not really intended to teach people to spell, but rather ultimately to read, and even to write. That is, we do not want to dwell on one word, any more than one note; we want people to string words together in a sequence like notes in a tune. And we want them ultimately to string sentences together, not exactly as they are in a sentence in an exercise, but as they ought to be in a serious sequence of ideas. As we want a person to play for pleasure, we want him to think for pleasure. And it is hard to believe that anyone can go on tapping one note or repeating one catchword for pleasure.

What is the matter with the curious cultural atmosphere around us is that it abounds, not in trains of thought, but in tags of language. Vast numbers know that a certain phrase should be used about a certain subject; but it never occurs to them even to wonder how it would apply to some other subject. There is such and such a set piece of argument against Pianos for the People, and such and such a set piece for Pianos for the People; or whatever the question may be. But it is rare to find any individual, on any side, guilty of the intellectual restlessness of asking himself whether the argument about Pianos for the People would also apply to Pianolas for the People, or wherein lies the difference of principle between pianos and bagpipes and guitars. To ask what an argument depends on; to consider where it leads; to speculate on whether there are other cases to which it applies; all this seems to be an unknown world to many who use the words of the debate glibly enough. The point is that they only use those words in connexion with that debate. They deal in formulas like those provided by the old debating club text-books; with A Hundred Points For and Against Home Rule.

Here is a phrase, for instance, which I heard the other day from a very agreeable and intelligent person, and which we have all heard hundreds of times from hundreds of such persons. A young mother remarked to me, "I don't want to teach my child any religion. I don't want to influence him; I want him to choose for himself when he grows up." That is a very ordinary example of a current argument; which is frequently repeated and yet never really applied. Of course the mother was always influencing the child. Of course the mother might just as well have said, "I hope he will choose his own friends when he grows up; so I won't introduce him to any aunts or uncles." The grown-up person cannot in any case escape from the responsibility of influencing the child; not even if she accepts the enormous responsibility of not influencing the child. The mother can bring up the child without choosing a religion for him; but not without choosing an environment for him. If she chooses to leave out the religion, she is choosing the environment; and an infernally dismal, unnatural environment too. The mother can bring up the child alone on a solitary island in the middle of a large lake, lest the child should be influenced by superstitions and social traditions. But the mother is choosing the island and the lake and the loneliness; and is just as responsible for doing so as if she had chosen the sect of the Mennonites or the theology of the Mormons. It is entirely obvious, to anybody who will think for two minutes, that this responsibility for determining childhood belongs inevitably to the relation of child and adult, quite apart from the relations of religion and irreligion. But the people who repeat these fragments of phraseology do not think for two minutes. They do not make any attempt to connect such a phraseology with a philosophy. They have heard that argument applied to religion; and they never think of applying it to anything else except religion. They never think of taking those ten or twelve words out of their conventional context; and

seeing whether they apply to any other context.
They have heard that there are people who refuse to
train children even in their own religion. There
might just as well be people who refuse to train
children in their own civilization. If the child, when
he has grown up, may prefer another creed, it is
equally true that he may prefer another culture. He
may be annoyed at having been brought up as a
Swedenborgian; he may passionately regret that
he was not brought up as a Sandemanian. But so he
may regret that he was brought up as an English
gentleman and not as a wild Arab of the desert. He
may, as (with the assistance of a sound geographical
education) he surveys the world from China to Peru,
feel envious of the dignity of the code of Confucius
or weep over the ruins of the great Aztec civilization. But somebody has obviously got to bring him
up as something; and it is perhaps the heaviest responsibility of all to bring him up as nothing.

I could give many other examples of this fragmentary sort of argument, which everybody quotes
and nobody develops. It is making, for instance,
the wildest confusion in the discussions about de-
corum and the dignity of the body. Any number of
people are content to say that the human body is
beautiful; though that argument would lead to a
conclusion which they themselves would regard as
rank lunacy. The true answer of philosophy and

theology is that there is nothing the matter with the human body; the trouble is with the human soul. But I am not so much talking about the true answer as about the absence of any answer. The point is that these people ask a question which they themselves are not prepared to answer, even along the lines which they themselves suggest. They only see the question as applied to some particular silly discussion about a French novel or an American ballet; and they never make any attempt to deal with the question as a whole. They only repeat the tame, controversial comment that is attached to that little local controversy. That is the thing which bears the same relation to thinking that hitting the same note on the piano a hundred and fifty times bears to playing in the style of Paderewski. We cannot all play like Paderewski or think like Plato; but we should be a great deal nearer to it if we could forget these little tags of talk from the daily papers and the debating clubs, and start afresh, thinking for ourselves.

III. ON A NEGATION

It is obvious that a materialist is always a mystic. It is equally true that he is often a mystagogue. He is a mystic because he deals entirely in mysteries, in things that our reason cannot picture; such as mindless order or objective matter merely becoming subjective mind. And he is a mystagogue because he sometimes actually hides these mysteries in mystifications. He pontificates; he is pompous; he tries to bully or to hypnotize, by the incantation of long and learned words, or by very simple things said in a very solemn fashion. That is the character of much popular science; at the best it is mysterious, and at the worst meaningless.

I never realized these truths so vividly as in reading the reverential report of an interview with Mr. Edison, the distinguished electrician, under the heading of "Do We Live Again?" It is possible, of course, that the distinguished electrician did not have much to do with it. It is possible that the reverential reporter is responsible for the form of it. To my simple mind it is not obvious that a successful electrician is an authority on the immortal soul, any more than that a successful military strategist has an ear for music, or an admirable French cook a grasp

of the higher mathematics. But it may be that the
air of authority here assumed does not come from
the electrician but from the journalist. Anyhow,
there is a very long and solemn encyclical that they
have somehow made up between them; and I shall
treat it as one thing. Whichever of them is responsible for the reasoning of the encyclical, I apologize
to the other.

I will begin with the smaller point of pomposity.
Mr. Edison as reported does not say much about
whether we "live again," but in a few well-chosen
words he disposes of the soul: "My mind is incapable of conceiving such a thing as a soul. I may be
in error, and man may have a soul; but I simply
do not believe it. What a soul may be is beyond my
understanding." So far, so good; all right; amen.
But I ask the reader to remember this agnostic statement in considering what follows. He then goes on
to deal with the origin of life; or rather, not to deal
with it. The following statement is of such fearful
intensity and importance that the interviewer prints
it all in italics, and I will so reproduce it: *"I believe
the form of energy that we call life came to the earth
from some other planet or at any rate from somewhere out in the great spaces beyond us."* In short,
there will henceforth be branded upon our brains the
conviction that life came from somewhere, and probably under some conditions of space. But the sugges-

tion that it came from another planet seems a rather weak evasion. Even a mind enfeebled by popular science would be capable of stirring faintly at that, and feeling unsatisfied. If it came from another planet, how did it arise on that planet? And in whatever way it arose on that planet, why could it not arise in that way on this planet? We are dealing with something admittedly unique and mysterious: like a ghost. The original rising of life from the lifeless is as strange as a rising from the dead. But this is like explaining a ghost walking visibly in the churchyard, by saying that it must have come from the churchyard of another village.

Then we go on in the same solemn and stately fashion. The life-force comes from some other planet, where life-forces grow on trees, or are chained up in kennels, and it pours itself into this planet, and particularly into certain things lying about, such as eggs. The interpreter becomes very ponderous and profound at this point. "What does this mean? It means, first, that, if Edison is correct, life is life wherever found." I think we may boldly commit ourselves, with a loud cheer of loyalty, to the proposition that Edison *is* correct when he says that life is life wherever found. Life is life, as here suggested, into whatever kind of egg it may enter, of the lowest sea-beast or the loftiest bird. That is, in our popular pre-scientific formula, as sure as eggs are eggs; or, in deference to the American literary tradition, as pigs is pigs. But while these rhythmic and recurrent phrases, that life is life, and eggs are eggs, and pigs is pigs, have something of the rounded beauty of song and dance and decorative pattern, they are not what you might call hustling in the matter of getting any further in the process of an argument. And Edison evidently has something a little more definite to say than the identical proposition which his interpreter holds up before us, like a scroll of revelation.

What he says is that eggs are all dead; and the same applies to seeds. He denies that there is, as many assume, a sort of germ of life in each. "A seed or an egg is merely a blue-print—an architect's plans for the building of a structure. It is as dead as any other blue-print. The energy that we call life flows into the blue-print and goes to work. If the blue-print was made by a rose-bush, the life-force makes another rose-bush. If the plans and specifications call for a man, the life-force makes a man." I am not quite sure where Mr. Edison imagines that his argument is leading him; but the only direction in which it could logically lead him is back to the oldest and most orthodox argument from design. The metaphor which he makes so important makes the whole imagery a little fanciful. Few of us walking in our gardens at evening have ever actually come upon a rose-bush making a blue-print, or even a red-print, or a green-print. And to believe that the rose-bush really does plan another rose-bush is to turn our garden into something of a fairyland. But if it does not, who does? The notion of a blind life in the germ did at least favour some vague evolutionary idea of a blind growth unfolding outwards into the void. But evolution has far less chance with the blue-prints of Mr. Edison. They are only an architect's plans: what architect's plans? It is the working out of a specification: who works out whose specification? So far as the argument has gone, it would seem that the reasoner has been forced to summon the aid of two mythological beings. One is a god called Life, who has winged his way from a strange star where such deities dwell, and who has the genius to understand and fulfil the most labyrinthine plans that he finds. The other is the Spirit of the Rose-Bush, a sort of dryad who draws up the most elaborate plans for posterity and leaves them like a last will and testament. Both of these figures, on the face of it, are far more improbable than the traditional truth in which most men have believed: that both were parts of the plan of a greater mind.

The philosopher seems to feel that he is becoming too much of a mystic, even for a materialist. In the next passage he treats the life-force merely as an instrument: "It is as if he had said that the electricity that prints a book might as easily have ground sausages if it had been applied to a sausage-grinder instead of to a printing-press." But a book does not print itself; still less does it print all by itself an appendix giving directions for the printing of another book. Still less does a sausage-machine grind out a specification of another sausage-machine. The electricity would not be applied to producing either books or sausages, if there were not a mind outside and above them: a mind that is neither a machine nor a book nor a sausage nor an electric current. His own analogy would prove that there is a mind behind nature, as there is a man behind machines.

Recoiling from this dreadful possibility, he falls back on a last fantastic theory. He says it is the cells that have souls. He says, again in italics: *"All cells apparently go consciously about it to reproduce the forms of life in which they appear."* I cannot italicize italics; or I would underline the word "consciously." Each one of the tiny cells in an elephant's tail has in its little mind a vivid and complete picture of an elephant. I will leave it at that. The article ends with the sad death of Mr. Edison's father at ninety-three; and the writer is quite sure (he does not explain why) that the old gentleman was thus cut off in his prime because the conscious cells found they could not come to an agreement. They seem to have taken some little time to discover their difference. But I only ask the reader to read again those words at the beginning: "My mind is incapable of conceiving such a thing as a soul." Is it so very much easier to conceive such things as these? Is it so very much easier to conceive a million souls, where we suppose there are cells, than to conceive one soul where we know at least that there is one mind?

IV. ON EUROPE AND ASIA

WITH regard to 'the opinion expressed by a very prominent capitalist that all might have been well in China if we had taken away the missionaries and presumably only left the merchants, I personally should say (as a slight amendment) that all might have been well if we had taken away the merchants and left the missionaries. But for that minor differentiation, I should be quite prepared to accept the whole substance and structure of his sentence.

But the text has in this connexion a further relation to the truth. I do not mean, of course, that the fault has been all on one side; or that there are no borderlines where the characters are mingled or exchanged. There may have been unpleasant missionaries who merely haggled and exploited like merchants. There are certainly unpleasant merchants who preach and moralize like misisonaries. But the general distinction remains; and it is one which must be, for any intelligent person, altogether to the advantage of the missionaries. If our civilization has anything to give the other populations of the planet, it must surely be a matter of giving a man ideas and not merely of selling him trousers or boots or a billycock hat. As it is, we have suffered from getting the Chinaman to change his hat without in the least changing his head; and have successfully sold him an English pair of trousers with an American revolver in the hip pocket. Our mood about the expansion of European methods in Asia has always been one of most muddled and immoral inconsistency. We have insisted on their having machinery and objected to their having machine-guns; we have often allowed them to enter the halls of our own national colleges and then forbidden them to take part in their own national councils; we have laughed at them for wearing their own costume and then laughed at them again for adopting ours; we have called the Chinaman a heathen Chinee when he was immovable and a Yellow Peril when he began to move; we have derided him for being deaf to Europeans and then accused him of lending an ear to Russians; and finally we express a reasonable apprehension about the destructive danger of his prolonged civil wars, and wind up by saying with a smile that they are never anything but sham fights. One does not need to be Pro-Chinese, still less Anti-European, to see that our neglect of Asiatic problems has here brought us into a rather hazy and irrational frame of mind. The Chinese question is really a serious question, and it is time the Chinaman was considered seriously as he is in himself and not as he appears to us, as the embodiment of something extravagant and extreme at the ends of the earth. I do not propose to deal here with any of the purely political questions of military or diplomatic policy; but I should like to suggest one or two neglected aspects of the philosophy of the whole matter; and to begin by saying that whoever else is right, I am quite sure that the eminent plutocrat was wrong, when he said that all the mischief had been done by missionaries.

There are two kinds of people in the world: the conscious dogmatists and the unconscious dogmatists. I have always found myself that the unconscious dogmatists were by far the most dogmatic. Thus there are wandering about the world, at any given moment, a very large number of unconscious missionaries. They do as a fact preach wherever they go; sometimes they are so fanatical as to practise what they preach; but they never know that they are preaching. They are under the extraordinary delusion that the thing they practise is universally regarded as practical politics. They imply by their every action a certain type of thought; though it is not a very thoughtful type of thought. Every gesture asserts a certain notion of social superiority; but it is a notion which they themselves have never very thoroughly thought out. And it is exactly here that the extension of the externals of our civiliza-ion is now breaking down. It is breaking down be-

cause it is external; and because it has been extended too far from its base. Most of the matters
involved did originally depend upon some moral or
philosophical idea when they first emerged out of
European civilization; but they do not know how
to defend themselves morally and philosophically
when they have wandered so far from Europe. Unfortunately, where they are insufficient, they are still
self-sufficient. They have forgotten their theoretical
basis; and are in the deplorably weak position of
being merely practical. They are dogmatic without
having a dogma.

In short, the European takes a superior tone; but
not about the things in which he is really superior.
In this matter there is a very queer irony and contradiction; and even a reversal of parts. Not only
has Asia borrowed all the wrong things from Europe, but Europe has also very largely borrowed
all the wrong things from Asia. To put the matter
in a compact and convenient material image, we may
take the question of vesture, especially in the religious form of vestment, and compare it with the
religious ideas that are behind the form. As a matter
of fact, the costume of many people in the East
really is much more beautiful than that of most people in the West. It could hardly be more hideous.
But it does, in fact, follow more of the free and flowing and yet traditional lines that are found in the

highest culture of Hellas and in all other humanistic moments of humanity. It is generally more natural and yet more symbolic than the costume of modern European people; or at any rate of modern European males. But that Asiatic element has never spread to Europe. There is no particular probability of stockbrokers in London suddenly appearing in the long peacock-coloured robes, that are to be seen on many Arabian beggars. It is not particularly likely that a banker in Birmingham will add to his dignity with a towering turban surmounted by a magnificent streaming plume. These things, in which oriental humanity has really remained more human, show no particular sign of spreading at all. The tendency, of course, is all the other way. It is the Arab beggar who tends to break out into the appearance of the stockbroker, at least in patches. It is the Indian prince who hastily disguises himself as the Birmingham banker. The very ugliest thing that our civilization ever produced, the costume and habit of the industrial nineteenth century in the big towns, that has really spread over the whole world, as Christianity has never spread, as chivalry has never spread, as monogamy has never spread, as democracy and the civic ideal have never spread. We have not succeeded in making the remote Asiatic feel like a Christian; but we have succeeded in making him look like a cad. This seems to me one of the strangest and most sinister of all historical contradictions; when we consider what Christendom has had to give, and what it has given.

But while this blight of vulgarity was spreading from Europe to Asia, something else was also spreading from Asia to Europe. And the strange thing is that this also was a blight. Its influence was not so immediately apparent, nor perhaps so widely distributed as the mere fashion of Cockney culture and commonplace clothes. But it has been considerable; and, as I think, very deplorable. What has come to us out of Asia, whatever else there may be in Asia, has been despair. It has been all those negative and anarchic ideals of disdain for the individual, of indifference to the romance of real life, of pessimism and the paralysis of the fighting spirit. It is ideas that have come to us out of the depths of Asia; and especially all the wrong ideas. I know, of course, that there are many other ideas in so vast and complex a continent; and many that are by no means so wrong.

But I am talking, not of the ideas that are deepest in Asia, of which I necessarily know little; but of the Asiatic ideals that have bitten deepest into Europe, of which I know only too much. And it strikes me as an astonishing antithesis and reversal that neither of the two great civilizations should have given its best to the other. We have given them a disfigurement; and they have given us a disease.

Now it is really in the matter of ideas that our own civilization is superior. There are some who do not believe this; because they always assume that deep ideas must be depressing ideas. They cannot bring themselves to believe, what is the truth, that the deepest of all ideas are inspiring ideas. Of those courageous and invigorating conceptions, the conceptions that make life possible to live, Christendom has had infinitely more than any other culture; more of the idea of free-will; more of the idea of personal chivalry and charity; more of the clean wind of hope. The metaphysics and morals of these things have been worked out by our fathers fully as deeply and delicately as any of the dark and disenchanted metaphysics of Asia. But the European travelling in Asia does not seem to know that he represents these things. He is still under the innocent delusion that he only represents some firm for selling hair-grease or golf-clubs. And when he comes back from the East he is quite as likely as not to be talking Eastern pessimism in the intervals of boasting of Western commercialism. Having never learnt his own religion, he is very likely to learn somebody else's; and that one which is really inferior to his own. If we consider these things, we may possibly begin to see a new meaning in the much-abused word "Missionary."

V. ON BROADCASTING

THE recurring discussion about the problem of
Broadcasting contains some sense and a great deal of
nonsense; and ranges from the admirably good work
of bringing consolation to the old and sick to the
wild absurdity of talking about listening-in to spectacles which were obviously for the eye and not the
ear. When a paper announces, "listening-in to the
launching of a ship," it might just as well talk about
"smelling a famous statue or eating a symphony or
examining a silence with a microscope. To listen to
the few confused and accidental noises that accom-
pany a great visual spectacle must be about as satisfactory as shutting your eyes and smelling all the oil
paints of the Royal Academy. On the other hand, the
more modest plea is a perfectly just and reasonable
plea. It is really true that Broadcasting can be used
to bring pleasure to those who are hampered in their
ordinary movements by age and sickness; and the
duty of bringing that pleasure, so far from being
nearly a modern scientific fad, ought to be recognized as a branch of the very ancient mission of human charity. It belongs to the spirit so nobly noted
in one of the oldest books in the world: "Eyes was
I to the blind and feet to the lame"; and there is no

man in that religious tradition who will say a word against it.

But I am rather inclined to think that a healthier society would regard these things as generally things for the unhealthy. It is a good thing to be "feet to the lame" in the sense of providing wooden legs and crutches to those who cannot otherwise walk about. But if we were to approach any athletic young gentleman of our acquaintance, and solemnly present him with a wooden leg, he would possibly regard it as an insult if he did not regard it as a joke. He certainly would not regard it as the next step in scientific evolution that he should go about adorned with three legs. It is a good thing to be "eyes to the blind" in the sense of providing short-sighted people with spectacles or possibly with telescopes. But it is not so tactful to insist on a beautiful lady with perfect and piercing sight wearing a pair of large goggles; or to provide her with a telescope to look at herself in the looking-glass. In regard to all these props and special supports of our bodily organs, we permit science to supply deficiencies; but not to imply deficiencies, and deficiencies that are not there. A healthier society may see that what is true of our physical organs is also true of our physical senses. The athletic young man ought really to be ashamed to sit at home and listen to a concert when he has only to walk down the street to find it. He ought to be still more ashamed to enjoy only half a play, when by walking out of the house he could enjoy the whole play. Such people are often criticized if they merely look on at athletic sports. They ought surely to be more criticized if they only listen-in, because they are not even athletic enough to look on.

I have remarked elsewhere that my own social ideal would admit many things as a sort of second best, which other social systems can only offer as the best. Just as we might give a man shares because we could not give him land, so we would give him a wireless set because we could not give him a walk. The change involves an altered attitude towards the modern worship of machinery; and the recognition of it as something really secondary to the much more wonderful machinery of the human body and mind. But it will be no disgrace to this branch of the science of electricity that it should take on the compassionate character of the science of medicine; or that the exceptional case should be cured by the physicist as by the physician.

I am not at all fond of regimentation or repression; that is why I have never written a novel about Utopia, as is the case with almost all of the sinful human race who have written anything in our time. Utopia always seems to me to mean regimentation rather than emancipation; repression rather than expansion. It is generally called a Republic and it always is a Monarchy. It is a Monarchy in the old and exact sense of the term; because it is really ruled by one man: the author of the book. He may tell us that all the characters in the book spontaneously delight in the beautiful social condition; but somehow we never believe him. His ideal world is always the world that he wants; and not the world that the world wants. Therefore, however democratic it may be in theory or in the book, it is always pretty despotic when it begins to be approached in practice through the law. The first modern moves towards any Utopian condition are generally as coercive as Prohibition. They are, as I have said, despotic because the whole design is despotic. It is despotic because it is a dream; and a man is always alone in a dream. All that we call Utopia is but the rather evasive and vague expression of the natural, boyish, and romantic sentiment, "If I were King."

Therefore, however ready I may be to explain what I would do if I were King to broadcasters and many others among my cowering subjects, I am very glad that I am not King. I do not seriously press my proposals for social management in this matter; and the broadcasters may breathe again. The millionaires and the men of science and the masters of machinery may take heart once more; for I have decided to let them live. But since it is so much the fashion to take a fancy and then describe it as a social policy, I do not see why I should not suggest this one, which I believe to be far more sensible than most. I would suggest that a really sane society will not further extend these extended communications; but rather restrict them. It will restrict them to those who really cannot do without them. It will refuse them to those who would really be much better without them; even if they were only better for the exercise of walking down the road. If they will not take the trouble to go and hear their own favourite public orator, I really cannot see why the public orator should come to them. Of course he does not really come to them; it is only a small part of him called his voice that comes; and many a politician will be all the safer when nobody can see his ugly face or criticize his shallow and shifty manners. The real objection to listening-in is that you cannot, however deep and earnest be your desire, tear a politician in pieces. But nobody, in any case, could expect the aged and the infirm to join in the happy youthful sport of tearing him in pieces. It is not a suitable game for invalids in hospitals or old women seated by the fireside; and if they enjoy the beautiful illusion of supposing that they will learn something about politics, by listening to political speeches, why should we not leave them their innocent dreams? And the more intelligent invalids, the more sensible old women, who wish to listen to good music, or even to bad, have obviously a claim on all Christian people to help them in their helplessness.

If Prohibitionists demand a medical certificate for brandy, why should we not demand a medical certificate for broadcasting? If a man must prove that he has a licence and a legitimate reason for importing large quantities of drugs, why should he not show a reason for dragging long streams of words through the air because he is too lazy to go and listen to them? If this sort of coercive collectivism is indeed our ideal state, cannot the police put a stop to the universal waste of crutches on people who are not cripples? Could not citizens be asked to make some effort to preserve the arts and institutions of the city in their old civic form? I do not profess any particular understanding of music; but I have some rudimentary understanding of patriotism; and the failure of the Queen's Hall Concerts does seem to me a definite disgrace to a great nation. I am told that people left off attending them because they could hear music on the wireless—heaven knows, not invariably the same sort of music. Now I cannot believe that all the audience of the Queen's Hall has been stricken with paralysis or now consists entirely of people who limp on one leg. And if they take it for granted that an art must always be enjoyed in the most comfortable conditions, as if they were the most inspiring conditions, I think they are wrong about the whole psychology of art. A man who climbs a mountain to see the sunrise sees something quite different from that which is shown in a magic lantern to a man sitting in an armchair. Let us be kind to the man in the armchair when he cannot get out of the armchair; but let us not assume that there are no peaks worth climbing or no theatres good enough to go to. I remember even in my childhood all the pleasures of going to the theatre; and one of the greatest pleasures was simply going there.

VI. ON AIDS TO GOLF

AMONG those remarkable "Sayings of the Day" that are quoted in the daily Press, I remember a sentence that is quite significant. Sandwiched in between two other epigrams, between Sir Humphrey Pumpernickel's paradox, "The British Empire must look to Britons for its defence" and the equally arresting *bon mot* of the Dean of Ditchbury, "True religion includes the desire for truth"—interposed, I say, in the same setting between some such jewels as these, I find a remark that really seems to me to be a text for the philosopher. I have forgotten who said it; but he was somebody of a social importance equal to that of the great men I have named. And what he said was this, or in almost these words: "The Charleston may really be of great practical use in teaching a man to be a good golfer."

Now that is really interesting; for it raises so many deep questions. First of all, would it be just as good if we said, "Golf may really be of great practical use in teaching us to dance the Charleston"? If not, why not? If so, have we established any principle by which we can distinguish between the primary and secondary aim? Why is one game good enough to be an end, and the other only good enough

to be a means to an end? Many men may regard golf
as an end. Some may regard it as a sad end; or even
as connected with coming to a bad end. Such was
the opinion of the Scottish minister; presumably the
only Scottish minister who did not play golf. Unless,
indeed, it was of himself that he was speaking in
hollow tones of remorse, when he said of the man
who plays golf, "He neglects his business; he for-
sakes his wife; he forgets his God." Some have held
that these three things are arranged in their order
of importance in the mind of a Scottish Puritan. But
I think this is unfair; and that the minister was only
leading up to a literary effect of climax. Anyhow,
God is an end, but Golf is not an end. It is just as
unphilosophical for a man to dance with a girl in
order to play golf as it is immoral for a man to desert
a wife in order to play golf. Girls are more than
golf-clubs in any rationally arranged hierarchy of the
creatures of God. And dancing is at least as good as
playing ball in any such system of relative values.
It seems to me, that, of the two, the reverse order
is the more reasonable. It really is, I think, more
sensible to play golf to perfect one's dancing than to
dance to perfect one's golf. Dancing has much more
approximate claim to be considered an end in itself
than hitting a little ball about with a long stick.
Dancing can be beautiful; and beauty can be an absolute; it can certainly be a joy in itself. I do not

say that I think most of the modern dancing I see is likely to be a diabolic distraction from the beatific vision; but that is a matter of particular taste and passing fashion. But certainly a man and a woman dancing might be something symbolical, spiritual, almost sacramental; certainly satisfying and complete. An artist could arrange a man and a girl in such a manner as to make a statuary group that could stand in marble and be immortal. But I am not sure whether the artist, in arranging a man and a golf-club, could satisfy his fastidious taste with any lines that would be at once light and final; living and yet eternally at rest. I can imagine him trying the golf-club at a good many different angles, before he got anything like a flowing melody in stone. The golf-club would give him no assistance anyhow; it could not arrange itself; while the girl might fall quite naturally into the perfect pose. Pure and absolute beauty is attainable by dancing, if not always attained by dancers. It seems clear that it ought to take precedence of what is solely a physical exercise, in any consideration of the means and the end. The ball-room where the Charleston is danced should stand at the end of the links and not at the beginning. The hero who hopes to hole out in one should be sustained by the vision of the more purely æsthetic sport. His long driving should be directed towards his late dancing. This is a normal and comprehensible order of interests. But it would certainly be most unseemly if he were suddenly to leave off dancing because he thought he had sufficiently reduced his handicap. It would be the reverse of a graceful group, in the spirit of perfect sculpture, if he were suddenly to break away from the girl and do a bolt for the door, from the feeling that he was now suddenly summoned to the higher duties of golf. He would be lacking in *finesse*, and in instinctive psychological sympathy, were he even to explain at length to the young lady that he was only dancing with her for the good of his golf. It would be almost better to rush madly away without any explanation at all; to leap wildly through the window and vanish in the direction of the links. But I am sure that arranging the ideas in this order reveals its insufficiency even in the practical manifestations of private life. It is more natural, even by the normal human habit, to treat the dance as pure enjoyment and the sport as having a little more of the character of the day's work. The very fact that the dance has generally come in the evening and the hunt in the daytime illustrates this instinct about it. The dance is in a double sense the end; it is something more like a termination and it is also something more like a goal or a prize.

I take this text because there is nothing about which men are now in such a muddle as about means and ends. Most of them have quite forgotten that there are such things. They not only put the cart before the horse, but they really believe that a cart is a mechanism constructed specially to draw horses. They not only empty out the baby with the bath, but they believe that a baby is a sort of secondary part of the bath-fittings made only to fit the bath. In all the current controversies people begin at the wrong end as readily as the right end; never stopping to consider which is really the end. A little while ago an intellectual weekly started an argument among the intellectuals about whether Man has improved the earth he lives on; whether nature as a whole was better for the presence of Man. Nobody seemed to notice that this is assuming that the end of Man is to grow more grass or improve the breed of rattlesnakes, apart from any theory about the origin or object of these things. A man may serve God and be good to mankind for that reason; or a man may serve mankind and be good to other things to preserve the standard of mankind; but it is very hard to prove exactly how far he is bound to make the jungle thicker or encourage very tall giraffes. Here again the common sense of mankind, even working unconsciously, has always stated the matter the other way round. All sane men have assumed that, while a man may be right to feel benevolently towards the jungle, he is also right to treat it as

something that may be put to his use, and something
which he may refuse to assist in definitely for its
own sake at his own expense. A man should be kind
to a giraffe; he should if necessary feed it; he may
very properly stroke it or pat it on the head, even if
he has to procure a ladder for these good offices. He
is perfectly right to pat a giraffe; there is no objection to his patting a palm-tree. But he is not bound
to regard a man as something created for the good
of a palm-tree. Nor is he bound to answer the question, with any burden on his conscience: "If there
were no men, would there be more palm-trees?" I
only give this as one example out of many, that have
caught my eye lately, of the fact that even thoughtful people seem to have forgotten how to think.

There are a great many other examples of putting
the cart before the horse or the means before the
end. One very common form of the blunder is to
make modern conditions an absolute end and then
try to fit human necessities to that end, as if they
were only a means. Thus people say, "Home life is
not suited to the business life of today." Which is
as if they said, "Heads are not suited to the sort of
hats now in fashion." Then they might go round
cutting off people's heads to meet the shortage or
shrinkage of hats; and calling it the Hat Problem.
They have already done this if not with heads, at
least with heads of hair. And if some of us ventured

to say that we thought that Eve's golden garment or St. Paul's "crown of glory" refer to a rather more elementary and eternal thing than the particular shape of hat to be seen in the shops for a month or so, we are rebuked as romantic and reactionary and very much behind the times. But this is an error. We are not especially behind the times. What we are is behind the scenes. And having been behind the scenes for a reasonable period, we know pretty well how often and how rapidly the scene-shifters shift the scenes. But anyhow we do not believe in re-building the whole theatre to fit one piece of paste-board marked Drop-Scene Between Acts IV and V; still less in rebuilding the whole world to suit the fashion of the theatre. We have adopted the habit of distinguishing the means from the ends.

VII. ON THE ENGLISHMAN ABROAD

It was an old objection to the Englishman abroad that he made himself too much at home. He was accused of treating a first-class foreign hotel as if it were only a fourth-class English hotel; and of brawling in it as if it were a bad variety of public-house. If there was a truth in the charge, it has since been transferred to a more vigorous type of vulgarian; and compared with a certain sort of American traveller, the English tripper might be mistaken for a civilized man. He has even taken on the colour of his Continental surroundings; and is indistinguishable from what he himself would once have described as "the natives." It might almost be regarded as a form of going *fantee*. But there is one particular aspect of the old accusation, which seems to me much more curious and puzzling than any other. It is that when the Englishman did blunder or bully, in demanding certain things merely because they were familiar, they were not really the things that had long been familiar to him; or to his fathers. I can understand the Englishman asking for English things; the odd thing is that it was not for the most English things that he asked. Some of the most English things he had already lost in England, and could hardly hope to find in Europe. Most of the things he did hope to find in Europe, he had only recently found even in England. When he asked for a drink, he asked for a Scotch drink; he even submitted to the intolerable national humiliation of calling it Scotch. When he asked for a game, he asked for a Scotch game; he looked to see whole landscapes transformed by the game of golf; which he himself had hardly played for ten years. He did not go about looking for cricket, which he had played for six hundred years. And just as he asked for Scotch links instead of cricket-fields and Scotch whisky instead of ale, so he expected a number of appliances and conveniences which were often much less English than American; and sometimes much less English than German. It would perhaps be pressing the argument fantastically far to say that even tea is originally a thing as oriental as hashish. But certainly an Englishman demanding tea in all the cafés of the Continent was as unreasonable as a Chinaman demanding opium in all the public-houses of the Old Kent Road. He was at least comparable to a Frenchman roaring to have red wine included in his bill in a series of tea-shops in Tooting. But I am not so much complaining of the old-fashioned Englishman who asked for something like the "five o'clock" which was recognized as English. I am rather complaining of a new-fashioned Englishman who would insist on American ice-cream sodas in the plains of Russia, while refusing tea because it was taken with lemon or served in a samovar. This bizarre contradiction and combination of the blind acceptance of some foreign things and the blind refusal of others, does seem to me a mystery to be added to what is perhaps the most mysterious national character in Christendom. That a man from Market Harborough should miss the oldest things in Old England, when travelling in Lithuania, may be intelligible and pardonable enough. That a man from Market Harborough should miss the newest things in New York, and be seriously surprised not to find them among Lithuanian peasants, is even more extraordinary than that he should want them himself.

But there goes along with this English eccentricity an even more serious English error. The things of which England has most reason to be proud are the things which England has preserved out of the ancient culture of the Christian world, when all the rest of that world has neglected them. They are at once unique and universal triumphs and trophies of the national life. They are things that are English in the sense that the English have kept them; but human in the sense that all humanity ought to have kept them. They are European in the sense of really belonging to the whole white civilization; they are

English in the sense of having been largely lost in Europe. And I have heard Englishmen boasting of all sorts of absurd things, from the possession of German blood to the possession of Jewish politicians; and I have never heard a single Englishman say a single word about a single one of these really English things.

One obvious case, for example, is that of having a fire in the old Latin sense of a focus. The idea of the hearth is one to be found in ancient Roman culture, and therefore in all the European cultures that have come from it. The idea of the hearth is to be found everywhere; but the hearth is not to be found everywhere. It is now most easily and universally to be found in England. And it is a strange irony that the French poet or the Italian orator, full of the splendours of the great pagan past, naturally speaks of a man fighting for his hearth and his altar; when he himself in practice has as much neglected hearths as we have neglected altars. And the only man in Christendom who really retains a hearth is one who has unfortunately rather dropped out of the habit of fighting for it. I do not mean, of course, that there are not really firesides scattered everywhere throughout Europe, especially among the poor, who always retain the highest and proudest traditions of the past. I am talking of a matter of proportion; of the preponderating presence of the custom in one place rather than another; and in this sense it is certain that it preponderates in England more than in any other country. Almost everywhere else the much more artificial and prosaic institution called the stove has become solidly established. In every eternal and essential sense, there is simply no comparison between that open domestic altar, on which the visible flame dances and illuminates, and the mere material habit of shutting up heat in a big box. The comparison is as sharp as that between the wild but splendid pagan custom of burning a dead man on a tower of timber, so that he went up to the sky in a column of fire and cloud, and the paltry paganism of our own time, which is content with the thing called cremation. Similarly there is about the stove all the essential utilitarian ugliness of the oven. There must always be something more magnificent about an open furnace, even from the standpoint of Shadrek, Meshach, and Abednego. Theirs was perhaps a rather heroic form of affection for the fireside. But, in comparison, we can all feel that there is something cold and desolate about the condition of the unhappy foreigner, who cannot really hope to sit in the glow of a fireside except by the extreme experiment of setting his house on fire.

Now I appeal to all those who have sung a hundred English songs, heard a hundred English speeches, read a hundred English books of more or less breezy or bombastic patriotism, to say whether they have ever seen the continuity of this Christian custom properly praised as a matter of pride among the English. And this strange gap in our glory seems to me another example of something that I noted recently in this place; the dangerous lack of an intensive national feeling in this country; and above all a much too supine surrender to other influences; from Germany; from Scotland; and above all from America.

I have taken only one domestic detail here, for the sake of clearness; but of course the principle could be extended to any number of larger examples of the same truth. The English inn, although a most Christian institution, was something more than an institution of Christendom. It was in its day a thing very specially English. I say it was; for I very much fear that capitalist monopoly and prohibitionist madness have between them turned it into something historical. It may be that the public-house will soon be dead enough to become a glorious historical monument. But the point to be noted here is the comparison with other countries, which had similar institutions, yet never had exactly the same institution. Sometimes, as in the case of the open hearth or fireside, they really had the same institution; and yet never had it so long. But anyone travelling in foreign countries can note that the new things are not erected on the basis of this particular old thing. We have spoilt the English inn; but at least we had it to spoil; and many national traditions, admirable in other ways, have had something much less admirable to spoil. In Europe, especially in outlying parts of Europe, we may see the latest modern machinery introduced without any of that intermediate type of comfort and convenience. The new American barbarism is applied direct to the oldest European barbarism. That interlude of moderate and mellow civilization has never been known. Men of many countries, both new and old, could only see it by coming to England; and even then they might come too late. The English might have already destroyed the last glories of England. When I think of these things, I still stand astounded at the strange quality of my countrymen; at their arrogance and especially at their modesty.

VIII. TWO WORDS FROM POLAND

THERE are certain things in this world that are at once intensely loved and intensely hated. They are naturally things of a strong character and either very good or very bad. They generally give a great deal of trouble to everybody; and a special sort of trouble to those who try to destroy them. But they give most trouble of all to those who try to ignore them. Some hate them so insanely as to deny their very existence; but the void made by that negation continues to exasperate those who have made it, till they are like men choked with a vacuum. They declare that it shall be nameless and then never cease to curse its name. This curious case is perhaps best illustrated by examples. One example of it is Ireland. Another example is Poland.

Within ten minutes of my stepping from the train on to Polish territory, I had heard two phrases: phrases which struck the precise note which thus inspires one half of the world and infuriates the other half. Most men have an immediate reaction to them, one way or the other; they think them spirited and generous or they would think them extravagant and futile. We were received by a sort of escort of Polish cavalry; and one of the officers made a speech in

French; a very fine speech in very good French. In the course of it he used the first of these two typical expressions, "I will not say the chief friend of Poland. God is the chief friend of Poland." And he afterwards said, in a more playful and conversational moment, "After all, there are only two trades for a man: a poet and a soldier of cavalry." He said it humorously, and with the delicate implication, "You are a poet and I am a soldier of cavalry. So there we are!" I said that, allowing for the difficulty of anybody having anything to eat, if this were literally true, I entirely accepted the sentiment and heartily agreed with it. But I know there are some people who would not understand it even enough to disagree with it. I know that some people would hotly and even furiously refuse even to see the joke of it. There is something in that particular sort of romance, or (if you will) in that particular sort of swagger, which moves them quite genuinely to a violent irritation. It is an irritation common among rationalists, among the drier sort of dons, and among the duller sort of public servants. It is one of the real working prejudices of the world.

Now if all those Polish officers had been Prussian officers, if their swagger had consisted of silently pushing people off the kerbstone, if their ceremony had consisted not in making good speeches but in standing in a row quite speechless, if their faces had been like painted wood and their heads and bodies puffed up with nothing but an east wind of pride, they would not have irritated this sort of critic in this sort of way. They would have soothed him, with a vague sense that that is what soldiers and men of action ought to be, or rather must be. I do not say he would approve of everything they did; but he would accept what they were. It would not anger him or even seem to him absurd; as it does to me, who belong to the other half of mankind. But what does anger him, what does seem to him absurd, is the idea of the soldier civilized, the man who is no more ashamed of the military art than of any other art, but who is interested in other arts besides the military art; and interested in them all like an artist. That the man in uniform should make a speech, and, worst of all, a good speech, seems comic, like a policeman composing a sonnet. That he should connect a horse soldier with a poet appears meaningless, like connecting a butcher with a Buddhist monk. In one historic word, these people hate and have always hated the Cavalier. They hate the Cavalier especially when he writes Cavalier Songs. They hate the knight when he is also a troubadour; especially when he always swaggers about with both rapier and guitar. They can understand Ironsides solemnly killing people in the fear of the Lord, as they can understand Prussian soldiers solemnly killing people in the fear

of the War-Lord. But they cannot tolerate the combination of wit and culture and courtesy with this
business of killing; it really seems to them provocative and preposterous. It seems especially preposterous when the Cavalier adds to all his other dazzling
inconsistencies by being quite as religious as the Iron-
side. The last touch is put to their angry bewilderment, when the man who has talked gaily as if nobody mattered except lancers and lyric poets, says
with the same simplicity and gaiety, "The one friend
of our country is God."

These critics commonly say that they are irritated
with this romantic type because it always fails; so
they are naturally even more irritated when it very
frequently succeeds. People who are ready to shed
tears of sympathy, when the windmills overthrow
Don Quixote, are very angry indeed when Don
Quixote really overthrows the windmills. People
who are prepared to give a vain blessing to a forlorn
hope are not unnaturally annoyed to find that the
forlorn hope is comparatively hopeful, and not entirely forlorn. Even the most genial of these realists,
Mr. Bernard Shaw, would be a little vexed if he
had to reverse the whole moral of *Arms and the
Man* and admit that the Arms counted for a little
less and the Man for a little more. He would be
slightly put out, perhaps, if the celebrated artillery
duel really took place; and the sentimental Sergius

blew the realistic Bluntzschli to pieces. But that is almost exactly what has really happened in modern Europe today. That is what happened, for instance, when the practical Mr. Broadbent went bankrupt in his other Island.

When the Poles defeated the Bolshevists in the field of battle, it was precisely that. It was the old chivalric tradition defeating everything that is modern, everything that is necessitarian, everything that is mechanical in method and materialistic in philosophy. It was the Marxian notion that everything is inevitably defeated by the Christian notion that nothing is inevitable—no, not even what has already happened. Mr. Belloc has put the Polish ideal into lines dedicated to a great Polish shrine:

> "Hope of the half-defeated; house of gold,
> Shrine of the sword and tower of ivory."

I am not dealing with such great matters, but describing an aspect and an experience; and before I leave these Polish cavaliers, I may remark that I had another chance of seeing them at the jumping competition in the Concours Hippique; and I will only mention one incident and leave it; for it is something of a parable. The course consisted of the usual high obstacles; but there was one which was apparently of a novel pattern and practically insuperable. Anyhow, one after another in that long procession of admirable riders, French, Polish, and Italian, failed at this final test till failure came to be treated as a matter of course. There were, of course, other misfortunes that were not a matter of course; even under the best conditions the race is not always to the swift; even experts on such occasions differ about the degrees of merits and misfortunes; and I am not likely to offer myself as an expert at a horse show. One of the lancers playfully asked me if I was going to compete; I made the obvious answer that, mounted on my favourite elephant, I would undertake to step over many of the fences, though certainly not the last fence of all, which I doubt if a giraffe could bestride. But the general feeling seemed to be that I should be more useful as an obstacle than a surmounter of obstacles; and that if I lay down on the course, it might be even worse than the worst obstacle. Otherwise I am an outsider in these things and only describe what I saw; and on that, as I say, even doctors may disagree. There was some amusement and some pity for one young Pole, who was, I believe, a novice or relatively untried person, whose mount in some fashion stumbled, so that the rider was shot over the horse's head. At least I thought he was shot over the horse's head; and then discovered, amid some amazing and jerky gyrations, that he was what can only be called clinging to the horse's ears. While the horse danced about the course in a *dégagé* manner, the rider seemed to crawl down his neck in some incredible way and rolled back into the saddle. He found one stirrup and tried in vain to find the other. Then he gave it up; the stirrup, not the race. He cleared a fairly low obstacle before him, and then, seeming to gather a wild impetus from nowhere, with one stirrup flying loose and swaying in the saddle, he charged the last impossible barrier, and, first of all that company, went over it like a bird. And some one said at my elbow with a sharp exclamation, in English, "That's just like the Poles."

Hope of the Half-Defeated; house of gold . . .

IX. ON NEW CAPITALS

I WONDER that no historian has written a great historical monograph bearing some such title as *The New City* or perhaps *The Second City* or more specifically *The City of the King*. Perhaps none of the titles fully explains what should be explained in the book. It would describe a certain action; which differed with differing conditions; but occurred again and again all over the world, or at any rate all over Europe. Briefly, it may be called moving from the old capital to the new capital. The old capital was naturally the seat of tradition, and generally of religion. The new capital was naturally the seat of fashion, because it was generally the seat of royalty. A sort of ancient archetypal form of it exists at the very back or beginning of the whole history of Christendom; in that great exodus of the Roman Emperor from Rome; the passage of Constantine to Constantinople.

The impression first struck me as I stood among the Baroque buildings and classical squares of Warsaw. But I remembered that I had something of the same impression and memory standing in the streets of Madrid. Warsaw and Madrid, at the two opposite ends of civilized Europe, both illustrate this curious passage in the history of our civilization. Both are practically products of the seventeenth and eighteenth centuries. Both are practically products of that "kingcraft" or sense of the supreme importance of the secular prince, which marked the time after the religious schism and the failure of the religious wars. The princes had so little link with their own past, and sometimes so much confidence in their own future, that they left behind them the sacred cities of the dead kings and the dead saints and heroes, as if they were nothing but cities of the dead. They began to build new cities of their own, for purely political or financial reasons; full of the rationalism of the Renaissance. These towns that were meant to be novelties are now necessarily much less interesting as antiquities. There is at least one Polish city much more national than the capital of Poland. There are several cities much more Spanish than the capital of Spain.

France is the working model of Europe; like a clock with the clockwork showing clearly in a glass-case. There the movements occur rapidly, sharply, and logically, which appear elsewhere more slowly, more confusedly, and more at large. And French history exhibits a sort of extreme case of this process. It was impossible to dethrone Paris; even by taking the throne away from under it, so to speak. But the eighteenth-century king did try the trick of taking the throne away; though he did not take it very far. He set it up in Versailles; and something in the proximity and the contrast exhibits more vividly than elsewhere the ultimate futility of the affair. Paris was far too powerful as the ancient popular and religious capital, which had once at the command of the populace shut its gates against the king, until he had returned to the religion. The populace continued to count even when the religion had turned to irreligion; it was still, so to speak, a sort of religion of irreligion. The French king went to his new town late; and he left it early. We might even say that he left it abruptly. We might confidently say that when he had left it, there was nothing left. The French Revolution was always regarded as an innovation; but it is worth noting that if it was the triumph of the new faction, it was also the triumph of the old town. It is curious that while the last court was being held amid the latest and most florid classical ornaments of the Age of Reason, the tocsins of revolution were being rung from old Gothic towers and the rebels were assuming, with deeper irony than they knew, the names of old fraternities of monks and friars. It is worth noting, I say, because what happened in the French Revolution has also happened in the more extreme example of the Russian Revolution. Even where the religion turns to irreligion, even where the irreligion sometimes turns to a sort of religion of devil-worship, the most ancient shrine and citadel in some mysterious manner retains and even recovers its power. Even for the desecraters of all shrines it acts as a shrine. Popular instincts return to it, even when worse or wilder instincts are let loose. The artificial creation of the last few centuries vanishes like Versailles in the conflagration. We no longer talk of St. Petersburg; we no longer talk very much even of Petrograd. The city of Peter the Great has lost its greatness; and once again, after many centuries, when we talk of Muscovy we talk of Moscow. Moscow is again, as the Russian poet said, the heart of Russia; even if the heart is broken.

These extremes are not felt in cases like that of Madrid or that of Warsaw; because the process was more natural and gradual and the nation more united and less challenged by internal hatreds. But even in the milder cases I should never be surprised to find that at some time in the future there was a return to the older civic centres. However this may be, it is certain that the older civic centres are generally the more interesting; and sometimes more interested, in the future as well as in the past. Now that Moscow has fallen to the Bolshevists as Constantinople fell to the Moslems, we might almost say of its fate, considered as a Christian capital, that both those imperial experiments have ended. We might almost say, in some mystical sense, that By-

zantium may yet go back to Rome. In the rising
fortunes of countries like Spain and Poland it is quite
possible that further resurrections may take place,
and that cities left for dead may begin once more
to live even a modern life. In the case of Poland, of
course, the more traditional and even mystical site is
the town of Cracow. It has always been, and still
is, of very great national and international importance as a University town. But it is also the original
Royal capital; and the seat of the kings at the moment when Polish kingship had perhaps its highest
influence in Europe. There still clings to it something
of the quality that belonged to a city of palaces as
well as a city of colleges or chapels. Warsaw has
become the modern capital of a republic; but there
still lies upon Cracow the shadow of a crown.

But what gives to Cracow a sort of sharp outline
of spires and turrets against the background of history is the fact that it is a seat of culture on the edge
of the uncultivated wilds. The city, like the nation,
is a sort of outpost, and the contrast is of the sort
that belongs to capes and islands and the edges of
things. That balance of the mind that we call philosophy is here balanced on the edge of an abyss.
That great gift of civilization which we call learning, and that greater gift of civilization which is the
art of carrying learning lightly, is here poised only
with a sort of perilous grace. The Germans, who do

not carry learning lightly and the wild Slavs, who do not carry it at all, press upon that more slender and subtle experiment with the weight of less living things. In Cracow can be seen all those crafts and schools of art with which we are familiar in the Western culture, in the free cities of Flanders or the cathedrals of Normandy. But we see them there thrust up against a vast and vague hostility which is something altogether alien to us and different from the internal quarrels of Flemish burghers or Norman knights. For centuries the Tartars rolled around these towers a torrent of Asiatic barbarism. There is little change in the position today; except that the barbarism is called Bolshevism. Sections of the city wall are still shown, which were guarded by the guilds, each lining its part of the wall; first the tanners and then the shoemakers and then the glaziers, and so on round the whole circle. Guilds of that type existed all over Europe; but when they went out to battle, it was commonly against other guilds or against the feudal nobility, as in the flaming victory of Courtrai. But here in Cracow the guildsman standing on that wall looked out across a wilderness that faded away into the formless east, where strange gods were worshipped under strange skies. Out of that mystery of the sunrise strange horsemen came riding from the legendary country of Cathay; and he felt himself to be in the ends of the earth. And from the tower of the city a trumpet is still blown every hour to the four winds of heaven, as if uttering the defiance of civilization besieged. Only the trumpet peal breaks on the last note; to commemorate a mediæval trumpeter slain by a Tartar arrow. And so odd and moving is the break that a man listening today can fancy that he hears not only the trumpet, but the bolt of the barbarian singing by.

X. ON THE MOVIES

THERE is a fault in the current art of the films which is intensely typical of our time. I have hardly ever seen a motion picture in which the motion was not too rapid to give any real sense of rapidity. For just as a thing can be too small to be even seen as small, or too large to be even seen as large, so it can easily be too swift to be even seen as swift. In order that a man riding on a horse should look as if he were riding hard, it is first necessary that he should look like a man riding on a horse. It is not even an impossibly rapid ride, if he only looks like a Catherine wheel seen through a fog. It is not an impression of swiftness; because it is not an impression of anything. It is not an exaggeration of swiftness; because there is nothing to exaggerate. It would be perfectly natural that the pace of such a gallop should be exaggerated; but it is not. All art has an element of emphasis, which is really exaggeration; the exaggeration varies with the type of artistic work to be done, as whether it is tragedy, comedy, farce, or melodrama; but the exaggeration may go to the very wildest lengths without necessarily losing this vividness and actuality. But when it goes past a certain point, in a certain direction, it passes a merely material border of the powers of the eye and the conditions of time and space; and it becomes not a rapid but rather an invisible thing. This would seem to be a very obvious piece of common sense in connexion with any artistic effect; yet these artists and producers, who talk so learnedly and work so laboriously, in connexion with artistic effects, have apparently not yet learnt even a little thing like that.

For instance, I have a simple, melodramatic mind; there is nothing lofty or peace-loving about me; and I thoroughly enjoy seeing people knocked down on the stage. I should have no objection to seeing them knocked down in real life, if the people were wisely and thoughtfully selected. In fact, I have seen them knocked down in real life; and sometimes knocked down very rapidly. It would be entirely in the right spirit of representative art if on the stage or on the film they were knocked down rather more rapidly than they can be in real life. But in nearly all those American cinema stories about "the great open spaces where men are men," my complaint is that when they begin to fight, the men are not men; but blurred and bewildering flashes of lightning. No man however slick, in no saloon however wild, in no mountains however rocky, ever moved with that degree of celerity to do anything. I therefore cease to believe in the man altogether; as much as if his body had visibly burst in two and the sawdust run out. He may be quicker on the draw than any other man in Red Dog Canyon, but I will be shot if any man ever shot or hit as quickly as all that. The principle applies to every sort of shooting. In one of Mr. Belloc's satires there is an allusion to an aristocratic infant who was "three years old and shooting up like a young lily." It is just as if the film were to take this sort of swiftness literally; and show the heroine rapidly elongating like the neck of Alice in Wonderland. It is as if the Coming of Spring were represented on the film in a series of jerks and leaps; as in that famous legendary landscape in which the hedges are shooting and the bull rushes out. In growing more rapid it would grow less realistic; and even if the bull does rush out, he must not rush ten times quicker than any bull is capable of rushing. We may well be content if he rushes about twice as quickly as the quickest bull in the world. But we, who sit watching these bloodless and blameless bull-fights, do not like to see the shattering of all conviction by mere confusion. We do like to fancy for a moment that we are looking at a real bull-fight; that we are contemplating a Spanish bull and not merely an Irish bull.

It is but part of the modern malady; the incapacity for doing things without overdoing things. It is an incapacity to understand the ancient paradox of moderation. As the drunkard is the man who does not understand the delicate and exquisite moment when he is moderately and reasonably drunk, so the motorist and the motion-picture artist are people who do not understand the divine and dizzy moment when they really feel that things are moving. Sometimes the drunkard and the motorist are blended in one perfect whole; and I disclaim all responsibility for the misuse of my jest about drunkenness, especially when it is combined with motoring. But the point is that there is probably an ultimate extreme of speed in which even a drunkard would enjoy nothing except a strangled sense of standing still. There comes a point at which speed stuns itself; and there is an unintentional truth in the exclamation of the radiant ass who declares that his new car is simply stunning. If speed can thus devour itself even in real life, it need not be said that on the accelerated cinema it swallows itself alive with all the suicidal finality of the hero who jumped down his own throat. Cars on the film often go much too fast, not for the laws of New York or London, but for the laws of space and time. For nature has written a Speed Limit in the nerves of the eye and the cells of the brain; and exceeding it, or even trying to exceed it, does not mean going to a prison but to a madhouse.

An artistic effect is something that is slightly impossible; though grammarians and logicians may both think this an impossible phrase. It is something that is mildly mad or faintly absurd. It is something that is just over the precipice of this prosaic world; but not far out in the void of vanity and emptiness. To accelerate a machine so as to make Mr. Tom Mix or Mr. Douglas Fairbanks run *a little* faster than a man can really run produces a magnificent impression; a theatrical effect like a thunderclap. To make him run a little faster than that destroys the whole effect at a blow; it merely extinguishes the man and exposes the machine. There is a figure in one of Michael Angelo's frescoes, in which the legs are somewhat lengthened so as to give an overwhelming impression of flying through the air. But if the legs had been extended indefinitely like the two parallel straight lines that could never meet, if they had wandered away in two endless strips over the whole of the Sistine Chapel, they would not produce any impression of rushing or of anything else. But the modern sensationalist has no notion of effecting anything except by extending it; by tugging its nerves out telescopically like some form of Asiatic torture; and increasing the pleasures of man by interminably pulling his leg. And that is why some of us feel the presence of something stupid and even barbaric in all this progress and acceleration; because it is but the elongation of one line and the exaggeration of one idea.

Speed itself is a balance and a comparison, as we

know when two railway trains are moving at the same rate and both seem to be standing still. So a whole society may seem to be standing still, if it is only rushing unanimously in a mere routine; for indeed the whole society which we call mankind is for ever rushing on the round orbit of the earth about the sun; but rushing without any marked feeling of exhilaration. The extension of speed in area, as well as in degree, is a way of neutralizing its full artistic effect. I have seen this error also on the films; when so many things are made to move and mix in the motion picture that it seems to be a whirlpool rather than a river. First it is all motion and no picture; and then it is not even motion because it is not even aim; and in all motion there must be the outline of motive. But I suppose that so very simple a blunder must have a rather subtle cause. Nothing is more curious, in the artistic history of mankind, than the obviousness of the things that were left out, compared with the cunning and intelligence of the things that were put in. It is a puzzle to understand how the splendid pagan poets of antiquity managed to get their effects with such few and vague ideas about colour; so that we do not always know whether they mean purple or blue or merely bright. It is equally a puzzle how the magnificent mediæval craftsmen could not see that their figure-drawing was as bad as their colour scheme was brilliant. All ages leave out something, which to other ages seems very simple and self-evident; and it seems as if this age would make itself a laughing-stock in turn to later times, by not seeing the most obvious of all the psychological facts in æsthetics—the principle of contrast. It will have failed even to understand that you cannot see a man run fast if you cannot see him at all.

XI. ON HELEN'S BABIES

AMERICA produced the first—one is tempted to say the last, but anyhow the best—of the modern works of light literature about the *enfant terrible*. It is almost a matter of religion that every infant is a terrible infant. Every child is, both in the most superficial and in the most solemn sense, a holy terror. But while all children are both amusing and alarming, while all children are therefore interesting, it can hardly be maintained that all books about children are interesting. But that original American work, which presumably set the fashion, was a thing genuine and convincing of its kind, and I fancy it has remained the best of its kind. Helen's babies really are babies, and (what is rare in fiction, as Stevenson noticed) they really are Helen's, though Helen never appears in the story. The temporary orphans do somehow suggest a mother who is not there. Anyhow, that very simple and sincere little sketch was interesting when it appeared, and it is interesting still, even if nobody is interested. If it has been forgotten, it has been forgotten for the sake of a swarm of plagiarists who have done the same thing much worse—who are, indeed, still doing it, and doing it worse and worse. A wholly alien idea of impudence has been brought in to poison the humours of innocence. Toddy and Budge were impossible, but not impudent. For impudence is not an element of the freshness of youth, but of the hardening of old age. The new people are not interested in the child, but in the spoilt child—that is, in the unchildish child. The whole point of the true tradition of the *enfant terrible* was that the child was unconscious and not self-conscious. The terrible infant is terrible like one of the forces of nature, like the blind sea or the random thunderbolt, laying waste the most elaborate social structures of man. There is in innocence a power of appalling indifference, of destructive detachment from all such elaborate social arrangements. It is like the old legendary theory of omens. It was essential that the oracular saying, the blessing or the curse, should be something arbitrary. It was best of all when it was something accidental. It must mean much more than it was meant to mean. It must be too great for the mouth that utters it; a man must mention a triviality, and other men realize that he has uttered a prophecy like the trump of doom. It was this random character in the thunderbolts thrown by that young god, the *enfant terrible*, that was the whole point of his legend. If he is only a little prig with several complexes and an ego, he is not the stuff of which myths are made. But the simplicity of the popular tradi-

tion, the tradition of the random word of innocence
as the rebuke to complexity, did linger in the little
book of which I speak, the best book of its kind that
I know. It is a curiosity of literature, or of ignorance of literature, that as far as I know nobody re-
members the author—I, for one, do not even know
his name.

But I mention that old American story with refer-
ence to certain criticisms of American conditions. It
gave, if only indirectly and by inference, a good deal
of information about the moral and religious atmosphere of that late nineteenth-century New England of which the religion was already changing,
but the morals remained the same. But the particular
point that interests me now in that connexion is the
celebrated remark of Toddy, the smaller of the two
boys, who could not be torn away from the con-
templation of his uncle's watch—or rather, of the
works of his watch—and who incessantly repeated
that he wanted to see the wheels go round. That
seems to me an excellent example of the unconscious
oracle of prophecy, of the random revelation of great
and serious things. Toddy did indeed make himself
a teraph-head, a blind mask and automatic mouth-
piece and the trumpet of the American spirit. That
is the whole meaning of industrialism, individual-
ism, progress, hustle, and hundred-per-cent efficiency. That is the meaning of Pittsburgh and

Chicago, of the sky-scrapers and the quick lunches. They want to see wheels go round, more and more wheels go round, larger and larger wheels go round, wheels that go round faster and faster. And this amuses them exactly as it amused Toddy, and for the same reason. It amuses them because they are as innocent as Helen's babies, even in a sense because they are as old-fashioned as Helen's babies. At bottom they have a simple conservatism—so simple that it does not even know it is conservative. It has hardly realized how much hustle is identical with routine. It does not know when its own argument is an argument in a circle as round as a cipher; and it talks about a hundred-per-cent efficiency without remembering that a hundred per cent of nought is nought. But Toddy is full of the fire of innocence, and has not wearied of seeing the wheels go round. He has not even discovered that it is the nature of a wheel going round to come back to the same place.

The notion that America is advanced only shows how deceptive is the mask of machinery and materialistic science. As a historical fact, those who have been advanced in their machinery have generally not been advanced in their ideas. In so far as there is any sense in the word, they have not been advanced either in the good or the bad sense of the word. The makers of machinery have been loyal or conventional or docile or servile, as you choose to regard it. The people without machinery have been intellectual, independent, speculative, or sceptical, as you choose to regard it. In liberty and detachment of the intelligence the old slow pilgrims race far ahead of the new rapid tourists. The flying-ships of Count Zeppelin and the petrol-traffic of Mr. Rockefeller are panting hundreds of miles behind the slow camel of Job or the white elephant of Buddha. If it comes to thinking, to questioning, to the use or abuse of speculation, no people have done it more than people sitting on the bare ground and staring at the stars. No people have done it less than people engaged in the applications of physical science to practical commerce. No people have done it less than the American people. The great mass of the American people remain, both for good and evil, stolidly, stubbornly, astoundingly conservative in their ideas.

As already observed, progress in machinery generally did occur where there was no progress in mentality. It was the reactionary countries which developed industrialism—the Germany of Blücher and Bismarck, the England of Wellington and Peel. It is one of the very few points in which England does resemble Germany, or some parts of Germany. That is why it was never mentioned by the Teutonists. It is also one of the very few points in which England does resemble America, or some parts of America. That is why it is never mentioned by the

Anglo-Saxons. The combination of Toryism in politics with restlessness in mechanics does really unite Berlin with Birmingham, and to some extent Birmingham with Bismarckville, Pa., U. S. A. People seem to forget that the very time when the English were introducing commercial industrialism was the time when they were actually persecuting political idealism. When a man was most concerned to get a living by being a manufacturer was the time when he might lose his life by being a Jacobin; and the six Acts restraining all liberty of popular protest were improvements that came in with the steam-engine and the spinning-jenny.

The desire to see wheels go round involves the idea that they will always repeat themselves. In one sense it may be called progressive, since when the wheels go round the cart goes on. In another sense it may be called conservative for in assuming that the wheels will go round it assumes that the wheels will not come off. But, above all, when the wheels are really going round rapidly they are generally in a rut. Industrialism is in a rut, and industrial America is rather specially in a rut; and none the less so because it can move in such a rut more and more swiftly. What the industrial spirit does not like is anything that cuts across that rut, that barges in at another angle. America is a very great living and complex reality, and everybody must apologize for having any impressions of it at all. But the only sense I can make of its present politics is something like this—that America is now the most conservative country in the world. It is resisting the spirit of revolt and novelty that comes from Europe. It is no longer a question of our calling in the New World to redress the balance of the Old. We are the New World, and we are upsetting the balance of the Old; and it looks as if the balance of America were a good deal upset.

XII. ON ELECTRIC HOUSES

I AM informed that there is an elaborately electrified house on view: a house in which the householder can be completely electrified; or possibly electroplated; or perhaps eventually electrocuted, which would seem a not unlikely refuge for anybody who had to live in that sort of house. Indeed, when I heard a lecturer a little while ago explain at some length (with the assistance of lantern slides) the complicated but complete apparatus of such a domestic system, I ventured to ask whereabouts in the electric house they had fitted up the electric chair. That would seem to be the most rapid and reasonable form of comfort in such a place. Or it might be useful for mild and well-considered experiments in murder, even before we came to the final experiment of suicide. The case for murder seems to me to be curiously neglected in the free and emancipated moral controversies of our time. I am perpetually being told that there are a number of hard cases arising out of the traditional respect for marriage. I could easily provide, from my own experience, half a dozen cases in which great discomfort has arisen out of the conventional prejudice against murder. I could give social instances which seem to cry out for assassination quite as pathetically as any that are supposed to cry out for divorce. Nor is it true to say that all such cases could be met by divorce or other division. Many are cases in which nothing but death could deprive the obnoxious person of his psychological or other influence over better people than himself. To give the names of those in my social circle, whom I mark out for extinction, would at present be premature and even embarrassing. But if I had a nice, neat, comfortable electric chair fitted up in my house, on the model of those fitted up in American prisons, I could quickly and quietly make a clearance of a great many of these social difficulties. It would be easy to receive a particular guest with gestures of hospitality; to wave him to a special seat with a special earnestness; to see him settled comfortably in it; and then to press a button with a smile and a sigh of relief. The hospitable gesture involved is not difficult. People often wave me towards particular chairs in their drawing-rooms; generally towards any massive seat of marble or granite, or to any cast-iron throne firmly clamped to the floor. And they always say, with a beaming smile, that they think it will suit me better. With heartfelt sincerity, I could say to the guest in question that I think the electric chair would suit him better. Difficulties might arise, of course, when he was dead; such difficulties have always embarrassed the moral reformer who assumed the specialist duties of the murderer. But, even here, electricity gives its ever-present aid. Obviously another button would be pressed; and the chair with its contents would sink through the floor, where the corpse would be mechanically ejected and consumed completely in an electric stove. Now here we have a real and serious social use for electricity; almost the only one I can think of, which could practically improve our present domestic life. But I cannot find a word about it in any of the accounts given to me of the Model Electric House.

That model house, I am informed, is described as the house of the future, dated less than a hundred years hence. I can imagine that even this prophecy might have its cheerful and enlivening aspect. The principle of comparison is often applied to our ancestors; and might equally wisely be applied to our descendants. We are often shown exhibitions of Elizabethan or Early Georgian domestic architecture, with the notion of suggesting to us how much architecture has advanced since those days. It is generally pointed out to us that many of the oldest English houses are only built of wood. It is generally *not* pointed out to us that most of the newest American houses are also built of wood. It is certainly not pointed out that these very houses that are now built of wood, are those in which there are most of the new electrical appliances. These things are not emphasized; because the object of the exposition is quite the contrary. We are shown the rude hovels of our ancestors, that we may be consoled by feeling that things might be worse even than they are. We are told that ancient Britons lived in low huts of wattle, or what not, that we may consider a brick villa in Balham is almost tolerable by comparison. In short, there are many who insist on all that was dark or gross or negligent in the conditions of early barbarism, so that modern civilization may for one wild moment take on a fanciful semblance of decency. But old things have to be made very black indeed, if modern things are not to look blacker.

Well, I cannot see why the same ingenious trick of comparison should not be tried in the case of the future as well as the past. As we produce an appalling picture of our great-grandfather in his hideous mud hovel, so we naturally produce an equally appalling picture of our great-grandson in his hideous electric house. Both will equally serve to raise our own spirits, and to lift up our hearts in humble gratitude to Providence, for the privilege of having been born not only after the former event but before the latter. I can imagine crowds of modern people coming away from the Ideal Homes Exhibition with beaming faces and rejoicing hearts, crowing aloud with pleasure or leaping and skipping lightly upon the road, at the thought of what they have escaped, by being born ninety years too soon for the Electric Houses. Surely anything that encourages contentment, and the reconciliation of men to their lot, is to be encouraged upon social grounds; and it is just as reasonable to teach unlucky people that they are lucky not to be their own descendants, as to teach them that they are lucky not to be their own ancestors. Neither perhaps will be wholly convincing or satisfying to a curious and inquiring mind; which might go so far as to demand that present conditions should be made decent in themselves, and not merely by comparison with the past or the future. But as an exposition of the comparative method, I can imagine few more effective than all this discussion about electricity and modern appliances. It is far more vivid and striking than the vague and dreary visions of the caves of the cave-men or the mud cabins of the peasants. The historical pictures of these past things are seldom detailed and never accurate in detail. They are not to be compared for a moment with the white and glittering nightmare of the steel house. The new scientific architecture can be perfected to a point of ghastly and demoniac ugliness towards which the dark fancies of our savage fathers would grope in vain, their legends were after all shadowy and unconvincing compared to our facts. None of those benighted slaves of mythology or theology ever imagined a hell to equal what the moderns have imagined as a home.

As to the confident assertions that these things really *will* be the characteristics of social existence a generation or two hence, I suppose we need not take them very seriously. People are always prophesying what will happen next; and they are always falling into the fatuous and obvious folly of making it merely the same as what has happened last. As the French king was certainly more powerful in the seventeenth century than in the sixteenth century, everybody would have prophesied that at the end of the eighteenth century he would be more powerful still. At the end of the eighteenth century he has ceased to exist. All the predictions of this sort are based on the idea that there has never been such a thing as a revolution or a reaction. Whether there will be a reaction against materialism before the date mentioned I do not know; and it is probable that I shall not care. By that date I shall have ceased to exist on this earth, like the French monarchy. For that alone I can be thankful for life—and death.

XIII. ON THE PILLORY

As a rule, those who discuss the good old days, and how bad they were, are a little vague about how old they were. They compare the modern clerk with anybody from a Blue Briton to a True Blue Tory, or the modern newspaper with anything from prehistoric carving to pre-Raphaelite painting. In a recent case which I have in mind, the writer fixed on a particular date in the past, for purposes of comparison; and rather a curious and interesting date too. He was concerned with some documents dealing with the years 1745–47; and told us the usual things about London being without lamp-posts, or having stage coaches instead of railway trains. And it struck me that it would make something like an amusing parlour game to compare notes about what ideas the mention of any date calls up in your mind or mine.

Now the first thought that actually occurs to me about the years 1745–47 has nothing to do with trains or lamp-posts. It is this: that those years mark more or less the last time in our history when any great estates were confiscated or any great lords suffered punishment for a crime against the State. The Jacobite nobles who were executed after the suppression of the '45 must have been the last of a long line of wealthy criminals or high-born martyrs who had found throughout the centuries that the law was higher than themselves. I am not exulting over their end; on the contrary, I am something of a Jacobite myself. I am only noting the fact that the taking of their lives and more especially the taking of their property, was the sort of thing that has not happened since. Other sorts of legal operations, of course, have happened since. The punishment of poor people, for the sort of crimes that are the temptations of poor people, still went on then, and still goes on now. But the idea of punishing a public man as a public enemy has, for good or evil, become an impossibility. And the idea of taking away the private wealth of a public man is equally inconceivable, especially if he is a really wealthy man. It is said that modern government makes life safer; and the claim is very tenable. But at least it is certain that modern government makes life for the governing classes safer; and never before in the whole history of the world has it been so safe a business to govern.

Let me take only one example actually mentioned in the newspaper article. Among the horrors of Old London, it mentions not only the absence of lamp-posts, but the presence of pillories. I have never been able to see myself that a pillory was necessarily worse than a prison. It need not in most cases be a more drastic punishment. It was certainly in all cases a more democratic punishment. A man was not only tried by his peers, but punished by his peers. It was no idle distinction; for he was sometimes acquitted and applauded by his peers. If a man were pilloried for a crime which the populace regarded as a virtue, there was nothing to prevent the populace from pelting him with roses instead of rotten eggs. In fact, I think it would be far from a bad thing if you or I or any ordinary individual were occasionally put in the pillory, to discover the emotional atmosphere of our social circle. Let us trust the experiment would be reassuring; it would at least be interesting and novel. The objection to the pillory suggested in the article consists in its ruthless publicity. But in the matter of punishment I am not reassured by privacy. I know that the most abominable cruelties have always been committed in complete privacy. I am not sure even about the punishments that are now hidden in prisons instead of being displayed in pillories. I do not say that we should do in public all that we now do in private. But it might well be questioned whether we ought to do in private the things we are so much ashamed to do in public. If there has been one respectable thing about the executioner, I think it is the fact that he was called the public executioner. I do not like his becoming the bearer of the bowstring; the secret messenger of a Sultan. But this is something of a separate question. It is enough to note here that there was at least good as well as evil in the publicity of the pillory. Indeed, there is only one real and unanswerable objection to the punishment of the pillory; and unfortunately it so happens that this is also the chief objection to the gallows, the prison, the reformatory, the scientific preventive settlement for potential criminals, and everything else of the kind. The only real objection to the pillory is that we should probably put the wrong man into it.

But let us consider for a moment the man who was put into it. Now nobody with an intelligent interest in the past, or an intelligent doubt about the present, would dream of taking the date of 1745 as the happy age to be regretted. It was a very bad period in many ways, possibly a worse period than our own; for many of the old humanities had passed with the common creed of Christendom, while many of the modern humanities had not come in with the French Revolution. The period, like all periods, contained very noble figures; but they were either defeated like the last Jacobites or detached and eccentric like Dr. Johnson. Its politics were, if possible, more full of knavery than our own. On the other hand, its commercialism, though already increasing out of proportion, was still more honest than our own. But no man who understands the disease of the present would look for the cure in that epoch of the past. He would seek for another social system in its days of strength and fullness; for instance, the best period of the Middle Ages. There again he would find the pillory; but my immediate interest is in the person he might possibly find in it.

Now a man could be put in the pillory in mediæval times for what was then called forestalling, and is now called making a corner. In some countries he could be hanged. There are at this moment walking about Europe and America a number of placid, well-fed, well-dressed gentlemen who boast of having made corners. Suppose I were to suggest that they should stand in the pillory. Suppose I were to suggest that some of them should hang on the gallows. Suppose I were to propose to punish them in modern times as they would have been punished in mediæval times; suppose that, and you will measure the whole distance and difference of which I spoke when I said that the really powerful man has never been really punished since 1745. There may be individual exceptions due to peculiar circumstances, but I cannot think of them at the moment. It is no answer to say that the powerful have not broken the law. Those who are powerful enough to make the law do not need to break it. The acts are not punishable in modern times which were actually pun-

ished in mediæval times. Nobody is so silly as to offer either period as a golden age; and there are real
superiorities in the more modern epoch. But I doubt
whether the matter is settled by pointing at a lamp-
post; and I fear it may merely serve to remind us
that the only tyrants who have suffered in our times
have been hanged on lamp-posts in revolutions.

XIV. ON FLAGS

In recent times the flags of all nations have tended to run to stripes, whether they were the narrow stripes of the American flag or the broad stripes of the French flag. Despite all we say, often truly enough, about the complexity of the modern world, there is a real sense in which modern things tend to simplicity; and sometimes to too much simplicity. In that fashion of tricolours which was started by the more or less rationalistic revolt of the French nation at the end of the eighteenth century, there is much of such harsh simplicity. There is something perhaps of the mathematical spirit of the pure logician; marching into battle under a banner that is like a diagram of Euclid. His nearest approach to heraldry is a picture of parallel straight lines which cannot meet. It is as if there were lifted above the lances and the sabres an ensign in the form of an isosceles triangle or a flag cut in a pattern to illustrate the square on the hypotenuse. That French flag of the three colours has been so gloriously coloured with heroism and martyrdom and the romance of revolution; with splendid victories and with defeats more splendid than victories, that it has become vividly romantic in retrospect; and more magnificent than all the eagles and leopards of the kings. But it is not at all improbable that those who originally designed it were men moving about in the cold innocence of the dawn of nationalism, who supposed that they were planning something as purely rational as the pattern of a machine. They may have cut up the flag into sections as they cut up the country into departments, ignoring the romantic traditions of the old provinces of France. They may have done it as calmly and confidently as they broke up the old crowns and coins of the great duchies into the exact equality of the decimal system. But romance has reappeared, not only in spite of the rational republic, but actually in the form of the rational republic. And the other nations, that have copied France in this as in so many other things, have varied the conception and the colours in ways that are more symbolic than anything required for the practical numbering of the nation. The black and gold and scarlet of the flag of Flanders carries the memory of the lion of Brabant; there is a significant hope of unity in the orange strip at the end of the new Irish flag; it might be called the Unceltic Fringe. And it was not for nothing, nor without another and even better sort of hope in the augury, that even into the new tricolour of Cavour and Garibaldi there crept a chivalric shield bearing the symbol of the cross.

Perhaps this modern simplification in political

symbols might be compared not only to the simplification in science but to the simplification in art.
Stevenson said that a geometrical problem was an
exact and luminous parallel to a work of art; and
many of the artists of his period undoubtedly loved
to simplify their art to such an extreme. In those
days the critics often complained that the pictures of
Whistler were mere bands of flat colour, a slab of
grey for the sky and a slab of green for the sea; the
whole having indeed something of the same flatness
as the flags. Whistler, that very militant person,
might well be said to have marched into battle wav-
ing a tricolour of grey, black and Chinese white. But
here again the same general principle holds; and
even simplicity preserved the tendency to variety;
and especially to national variety. It was soon found
that character could not be simplified for nothing
or rationalized out of existence. And in no case was
this more marked than in the very countries where
science was supposed to be most abstract or art most
impersonal. Nothing, for instance, could be more
impersonal than impressionism; but anybody studying its origins will receive a very French impression. Both in science and art it was found that even
a universal simplification did not get rid of a fundamental division, like the three divisions in the
simplest tricolour flag.

But there is a special truth in this symbol which

specially affects the intercourse of nations. It may
be stated under the same figure of speech. The Bel-
gian flag may be, as Whistler would put it, an arrangement in black and yellow and red, or the Italian a different effect produced by the introduction
of white and green. But there are flags that are
arrangements in the same colours; only that they
are differently arranged. And this is perhaps the
nearest metaphor by which we can describe a very
vital and even dangerous similarity and dissimilarity.
The French republican flag is of red, white, and
blue; but so, for that matter, is the Union Jack; so
also is the Stars and Stripes. When Napoleon forced
the English out of Toulon, when Nelson broke the
French at Trafalgar, the glorious battle-flags reared
against each other in that heroic combat were both
tricolours of the same blended hues. When the victory of the *Chesapeake* raised Old Glory for a moment above the mistress of the seas, it was still a new
flag but an old tricolour. And the hearty old English
Tories, who loved to sing over their port the patriotic
song which ran "Three Cheers for the Red, White,
and Blue," would have been considerably annoyed,
not to say agitated, if some polite Frenchman had
bowed in acknowledgment of this compliment to the
Republic and the Revolution. They would have been
still more annoyed if some breezy and brotherly
Anglo-Saxon from Alabama had expressed his grati-

fication at finding that the old country had got wise
to the go-ahead virtues of the Stars and Stripes. All
the colours would indeed be the same; all would be
familiar with the look of blue or red; and any Anglo-
Saxon might, if he liked, compare the blue to the
sea which was common to the two nations or the red
to the blood that is thicker than water. But the fact
remains that what affects people in practice is not
the tints they use but the pictures that they make.
In this sense form is much more powerful than colour. Men see a sign, an emblem, an object, before
they see the polychrome elements that make it up.
And, as I have already suggested, these things are an
allegory.

What affects men sharply about a foreign nation
is not so much finding or not finding familiar things;
it is rather not finding them in the familiar place. It is
not so much that he cannot find red, white, and
blue on the French or American flag; but that he
always finds red where he expects blue and blue
where he expects white. The actual mixture of human
and ethical elements in the different countries is not
so very different. The amount of good and evil is
pretty much what it is everywhere in the moral
balance and mortal battle of the soul of man. In
that sense we may say that every nation is an arrangement in black and white. Perhaps it is rather like an
unkind historical allusion to say that American his-

tory has been written in black and white. And yet
that historical allusion would be an excellent historical illustration. All through the eighteenth and early
nineteenth centuries America and England were as-
tonished at each other; not because either was complete or consistent, but because each had inequality
where the other expected equality. The English knew
that they had not got rid of a squirearchy, which
many of them already wanted to get rid of; but
they said to themselves with satisfaction that if they
had squires, at least they did not have slaves. The
Americans admitted that they had not got rid of the
slaves; many of them admitted it with regret or
shame; but they felt that if they had slaves, at least
they also had citizens. They felt that, in comparison,
England had no notion even of the nature of citizens. These cross purposes can be seen in the great
national figures of both nations. An advanced demo-
crat like Jefferson still has slaves. An antiquated
Tory like Johnson is yet horrified at slavery. But
Jefferson could not conceive how Johnson could sub-
mit to an old fool like George III. Still less could
he understand the acceptation of aristocracy; as little as the other could understand the acceptation of
slavery. We might almost say that in the one case
there were lords and no slaves and in the other
slaves and no lords. But that sort of misunderstanding always perplexes the mutual understanding of

nations. And in no case is this stronger than in the present relations of England and America. I have deliberately taken an old and familiar example, as I have taken an obvious and popular metaphor, to make clear this point about the difference between elements and the relation of elements, between colours and the arrangement of colours. And in these days when people are talking so much about the necessity of peace and international sympathy, I suggest it as one of the problems on which there has been much talking and perhaps not quite enough thinking.

XV. ON SENTIMENT.

In reading some recent discussions about Victorian fiction I have come upon a curious fallacy about what is called sentiment. It is generally called sentimentalism or sentimentality. The term, in any case, is always applied in a bad sense. And it is almost always applied exactly where it does not apply. There are apparently some people so constituted that they are sickened by any sentiment concerned with certain simple and popular things; such as the love of mothers or the charm of children. They wince at the very word "mother"; and quiver with intellectual disgust at the very mention of any such sentiment as "women and children first." But this sort of fastidiousness or disdain is the very opposite of what it professes to be. So far from being an attack on sentiment it is itself an excess of sensibility. It has the supreme sentimental fault of being affected by the mere associations of words, instead of by the intrinsic idea in things. There is nothing of illusion, or even of superficiality, in recognizing the importance of the emotions belonging to these things. There is nothing weak about showing such feelings; there is nothing realistic about denying such feelings. The feelings are facts; they are even very fundamental facts. We are not the less dealing with facts, because we are dealing with a very large number of facts. You may be so constituted, in your nervous system, that what is common rapidly becomes commonplace. But that is because your emotions are easily exhausted; not because the subject is exhausted. Your attitude is really and truly sentimental; because it is subjective. It is affected by repetition; but it is not in touch with the reality about the things repeated. As an objective fact, the hundredth blade of grass is as green as the first blade of grass. The hundredth sunbeam is as bright as the first sunbeam. And the hundredth child murdered by King Herod is as pathetic as the first. King Herod may have come to the end of his pleasure; but the mother has not come to the end of her pain. And her pain is a plain fact of nature, absolutely radical and realistic; as solid as a lump of rock. It has every quality of stone; antiquity, universality, simplicity, permanence. And a stone is not any the less a stone because it is not the only pebble on the beach.

It is obvious that anti-sentimentalism is only a rather priggish and a rather snobbish form of sentimentalism. The fastidious person is really preferring feelings to facts. Nevertheless, we all know that there is something weak and deleterious that deserves to be called sentimentalism. Only, as is commonly the case today, hardly anybody makes any attempt at defining the thing he is always denouncing; finding it much easier to denounce than to define. I will not claim a final definition here; but I will suggest a principle as a practical test. The sin of sentimentalism only occurs when somebody indulges a feeling, sometimes even a real feeling, at the prejudice of something equally real, which also has its rights. The most common form of this dishonesty is what is called "having it both ways." I have always felt it in the conventionalized laxity of fashionable divorce; where people want to change their partners as rapidly as at a dance, and yet want again and again to thrill at the heroic finality of the sacramental vow, which is like the sound of a trumpet. They want to eat their wedding cake and have it.

It is as healthy to enjoy sentiment as to enjoy jam. In the evil of sentimentalism there must always be some suggestion of *stealing* jam. It has many milder forms and lighter occasions than those above mentioned, which I am not going to debate again. All that concerns me here is the general definition; that the evil is not in the recognition of the feeling as a fact; or even in the enjoyment of the feeling as a fact; it is in the destruction or the dishonouring of some other fact. It is in the attempt to combine a fact and falsehood in one act of the mind. It is not silly to think that a young soldier looks splendid with a plume or a sword, riding away to the tune of

"The Girl I Left Behind Me." Soldiers do go to battle and do leave girls behind; and the passions involved are not only romantic but real. But if we then make fancy pictures of war, and refuse to admit that wounds hurt, or that heroes can be killed, or that good causes can be defeated, then we are trying to hold two contrary conceptions in the mind at once. We want to admire the soldier and deny what is admirable in him.

In connexion with Victorian literature, I will take a popular example; a play which everybody knows, which nearly everybody enjoys and admires; which I certainly heartily enjoy and admire; but which has not escaped the charge of sentimentality. And what strikes me as odd is that it is blamed where it does not fail, and not half so much blamed where it does. I mean Sir James Barrie's famous fantasia of "Peter Pan." I am not dealing with the aspect of it that I like most; the pirate with the hook or the crocodile with the clock inside it. It would surely be an excess of sensibility to see anything particularly sentimental about them. But many sensible people have complained very scornfully of the opening of the final scene; of the bereaved mother moving sadly about the room or playing soft music on the piano. I am not sure that I agree with this complaint; though of course it depends how the thing is done. But real sentimentalism is a sin against reality; and

this is not really a sin against reality. Mothers do
miss their children; a mother probably would think
of them with affection if the house were suddenly
empty; possibly with more affection than at those
exciting moments when it seems a little too full.
Some ladies do play on pianos, though the taste is
doubtless liable to abuse; and music is a perfectly
genuine way of relieving the emotions. There is
nothing really false in all this; and indeed the critics
do not really mean that it is false, but only that it is
familiar. Yet there is something that does ring false
in the play, and it seems to have been much less
criticized. The final decision of Peter Pan was a
bad example of having it both ways. What is really
wrong with that delightful masterpiece is that the
master asked a question and ought to have answered
it. But he could not bring himself to answer it; or
rather he tried to say yes and no in one word. A
very fine problem of poetic philosophy might be
presented as the problem of Peter Pan. He is represented as a sort of everlasting elf, a child who
never changes age after age, but who in this story
falls in love with a little girl who is a normal person.
He is given his choice between becoming normal with
her or remaining immortal without her; and either
choice might have been made a fine and effective
thing. He might have said that he was a god, that
he loved all but could not live for any; that he

belonged not to them but to multitudes of unborn babes. Or he might have chosen love, with the inevitable result of love, which is incarnation; and the inevitable result of incarnation, which is crucifixion; yes, if it were only crucifixion by becoming a clerk in a bank and growing old. But it was the fork of the road; and even in fairyland you cannot walk down two roads at once. The one real fault of sentimentalism in this fairy play is the compromise that is ultimately made; whereby he shall go free for ever but meet his human friend once a year. Like most practical compromises, it is the most unpractical of all possible courses of action. Even the baby in that nursery could have seen that Wendy would be ninety in no time, after what would appear to her immortal lover a mere idle half-hour. But I only mention it here as the first example that occurs to me of the sentimental fault where it really exists; and the way in which it is often alleged where it does not exist. It is not sentimental, in the bad sense, to make a mother play on a piano; because the notes on a piano only profess to be notes and not words that define and decide. But it is sentimentalism to use words in order to confuse and weaken, when they ought to define and decide. It is not sentimental to deal with things of sentiment such as tone or melody or minor graces of life. It is not false to be sentimental about these things that are avowedly things of sentiment. The evil comes in when we waver about weighty matters; not when we allow gossamer and thistledown to follow their own nature, which is to waver. And it may be noted that many great periods in the past, strong in arms and in counsel, gaining triumphs and building codes of law, reconstructing civilization or reawakening religion, were none the less very sentimental about lesser and lighter things. The great days of the Grand Siècle, of the Revolution, and of Napoleon were full of china shepherdesses and little opera tunes. But the great men of those days did not hesitate between the King and the Republic as we hesitate between a hundred new religions and stale philosophies. There is nothing feeble-minded about playing the flute, considered as playing the flute. But if the trumpet give an uncertain sound, who shall prepare himself for the battle?

XVI. ON MISUNDERSTANDING

A NEWSPAPER comment on something I recently wrote has given me a momentary illusion of having really got hold of what is the matter with modernity. For that serpent is as slippery as an eel, that demon is as elusive as an elf. But for the moment I thought I had him—or at least a perfect specimen of him. I wrote recently to the effect that music at meals interferes with conversation. And certain people at once began to discuss whether music at meals interferes with digestion. And in that one detail I seemed to have caught the very devil himself by the tail.

Those who read my article know that I never even mentioned digestion. I never even thought of it. It never crosses my mind while I am eating meals. It certainly never crosses my mind when I am listening to music. Least of all did it ever cross my mind while I was writing that particular article. And the idea that it should cross anybody's mind, not to say occupy anybody's mind, in connexion with the other controversy seems to me a compendium of all the dullness, baseness, vulgarity, and fear that make up so much of the practical philosophy of this enlightened age. What I complained of was not that music interfered with animal assimilation, but that it interfered with human speech, with the talk of taverns like the Tabard or the Mermaid, with the talk of Dr. Johnson or Charles Lamb, with the *Noctes Ambrosianæ* or the Four Men of Sussex; with all the ancient Christian custom of men arguing each other's heads off and shouting each other down for the glory of reason and the truth. Those great talkers no more thought about their digestion at dinner than the heroes of the Iliad or the Song of Roland felt their own pulses and took their own temperatures in the thick of the battle. It is true that I did not confine myself to complaining of meals being spoilt by music. I also complained of music being spoilt by meals. I was so impertinent as to suggest that if we want to listen to good music we should listen to it, and honour it with our undivided attention. A fine musician might surely resent a man treating fine music as a mere background to his lunch. But a fine musician might well murder a man who treated fine music as an aid to his digestion.

But what interests me is this swift, unconscious substitution of the subject of digestion, which I had never mentioned, for the subject of human intercourse, which I had. It has hidden in it somewhere a sort of secret of our social and spiritual abnormality. It is a sort of silent signal of all that has gone wrong with our brains and tempers and memories and hearts

—and also, doubtless, digestions. It is so significant that it is worth while to attempt to resolve it into the elements that make it the monstrous and ominous thing it is. Before this evil and elusive creature escapes me once more, I will attempt to dissect it and make a sort of diagram of its deformities.

First, there is that stink of stale and sham science which is one of the curses of our times. The stupidest or the wickedest action is supposed to become reasonable or respectable, not by having found a reason in scientific fact, but merely by having found any sort of excuse in scientific language. This highly grotesque and rather gross topic is supposed to take on a sort of solemnity because it is physiological. Some people even talk about proteids, vitamins—but let us draw a veil over the whole horrid scene. It is enough to note that one element in the hideous compound is a love of talking about the body as a scientific thing— that is, talking about it as if it were a serious thing.

Next, there is a morbidity and a monstrous solitude. Each man is alone with his digestion as with a familiar demon. He is not to allow either the wine or the music to melt his soul into any sociable spirit of the company. Wine is bad for his digestion and music is good for his digestion. He therefore abstains from the one and absorbs the other in the same inhuman isolation. Diogenes retired into a tub and St. Jerome into a cave; but this hermit uses his own inside as his cavern—every man is his own cask, and it is not even a wine-cask.

Third, there is materialism or the very muddiest sort of atheism. It has the obscure assumption that everything begins with the digestion, and not with the divine reason; that we must always start at the material end if we wish to work from the origins of things. In their hapless topsy-turvy philosophy, digestion is the creator and divinity the creature. They have at the back of their minds, in short, the idea that there is really nothing at the back of their minds except the brute thing called the body. To them, therefore, there is nothing comic or incongruous about saying that a violin solo should be a servant of the body or of the brute; for there is no other god for it to serve.

There also hides in the heart of this philosopher the thing we call hypochondria and a paralysing panic. I have said that it serves the body; but many men in many ages have served their bodies. I doubt if any men in any ages were ever so much afraid of their bodies. We might represent in some symbolic drama a man running down the street pursued by his own body. It is inadequate to say of this sort of thing that it is atheism; it would be nearer the truth to say it is devil-worship. But they are not even the red devils of passion and enjoyment. They are really only the blue devils of fear.

Then there is what there always is in such philosophy, the setting of the cart to draw the horse. They do not see that digestion exists for health, and health exists for life, and life exists for the love of music or beautiful things. They reverse the process and say that the love of music is good for the process of digestion. What the process of digestion is ultimately good for they have really no idea. I think it was a great mediæval philosopher who said that all evil comes from enjoying what we ought to use and using what we ought to enjoy. A great many modern philosophers never do anything else. Thus they will sacrifice what they admit to be happiness to what they claim to be progress; though it could have no rational meaning except progress to greater happiness. Or they will subordinate goodness to efficiency; though the very name of good implies an end, and the very name of efficiency implies only a means to an end. Progress and efficiency by their very titles are only tools. Goodness and happiness by their very titles are a fruition; the fruits that are to be produced by the tools. Yet how often the fruits are treated as fancies of sentimentalism and only the tools as facts of sense. It is as if a starving man were to give away the turnip in order to eat the spade; or as if men said that there need not be any fish, so long as there were plenty of fishing-rods. There is all that queer inversion of values in talking about

music as an aid not only to dinner, but even to the
digestion of dinner.

There is more generally a flat, unlifted, unlaugh-
ing spirit, that can accept this topsy-turvydom without even seeing that it is topsy-turvy. It does not even
rise high enough to be cynical. It does not utter its
materialistic maxim even as a pessimist's paradox.
It does not see the joke of saying that the Passion
Music can assist a gentleman to absorb a veal cutlet,
or that a Mass of Palestrina might counteract the
effects of toasted cheese. What is said on this subject is said quite seriously. That seriousness is perhaps the most frivolous thing in the whole of this
frivolous society. It is a spirit that cannot even rouse
itself enough to laugh.

In short, it is the magic of that one trivial phrase,
about music and digestion, that it calls up suddenly
in the mind the image of a certain sort of man, sitting at a table in a grand restaurant, and wearing a
serious and somewhat sullen expression. He is mani-
festly a man of considerable wealth; and beyond
that he can only be described by a series of negatives.
He has no traditions, and therefore knows nothing
of the great traditional talking that has enriched our
literature with the nights and feasts of the gods. He
has no real friends, and therefore his interests are
turned inwards, but more to the state of his body than
of his soul. He has no religion, and therefore it comes

natural to him to think that everything springs from a material source. He has no philosophy, and therefore does not know the difference between the means and the end. And, above all, there is buried deep in him a profound and stubborn repugnance to the trouble of following anybody else's argument; so that if somebody elaborately explains to him that it is often a mistake to combine two pleasures, because pleasures, like pains, can act as counter-irritants to each other, he only receives the vague impression that somebody is saying that music is bad for his digestion.

XVII. ON BUDDHISM

"An English Buddhist," the author of a very valuable and lucid essay on the real nature of Buddhism in the *Buddhist Annual* of Ceylon, seems to me to be a rather disconcerting ally for most other English Buddhists. At least, he would hardly be popular with those English Buddhists who more often call themselves Theosophists. The nearest Theosophy can come to being a popular religion is a romance of reincarnation. In other words, it is a romance about the soul remaining immortally itself, through the disguises of many different lives. The "English Buddhist" not only denies this immortality of the soul, but he denies the very existence of the soul. Indeed he denies the very existence of the self. Existence is simply a destructive cataract of perpetually disappearing thoughts and feelings, at no moment of which can anybody be said to possess anything, least of all a personality. As nobody has any personality, naturally nobody has any personal immortality. Indeed, the writer begins with a series of spirited and trenchant negatives. They at least refreshingly remind us that the English Buddhist is a very English Buddhist. He is anxious to maintain that Buddhism did not begin with Asiatics, but with "men of the Aryan race"; and certainly there is something in his own tone of the fighting spirit of the European. I hope he will allow another man of Aryan race, who prefers to call himself a European and a Christian, to quote in order his clear statements about Buddhism, and to append to each of them the obvious comment of Christianity. First, he says of Buddhism, "It is not a worship of the Buddha": in other words, it does not give men anybody or anything to worship. Second, "It is not any form of Pantheism": that is, it is not any form of theism; it has no God and certainly none so healthy as Pan. Third, "It has nothing to do with any theories of the origin of the Universe": that is, it does not satisfy the immortal intellectual curiosity of man about the origin of the Universe. Fourth, "It is not a body of dogma to be received as faith, on the authority of the Buddha, or of anyone else": no, it is a body of doubts to be entertained about everybody, including the Buddha and everybody else. Fifth, "It contains no esoteric mysteries": that is, it contains nothing of what nearly all our Theosophists meant when they called themselves Esoteric Buddhists. Sixth, "It does not teach the transmigration of souls": that is, it does not teach the one thing which nearly all its teachers in this country have especially recommended it as teaching. Seventh, "It contains no system or college of 'priests,' for there are no priestly functions to perform": in other words, there are no practical functions to perform. There is nothing for anybody to give to anybody; nothing for anybody to do for anybody; no substance or support that anybody has in store for anybody; no daily bread, no pardon of trespasses, and no deliverance from evil.

Thus does the English Buddhist make a sweeping and ruthless clearance of the whole of Buddhism as commonly offered to the English. Of the extraordinary thing that he offers instead I will say something in a moment. But let me pause, before passing on, upon one of these very rapid but very rigid repudiations—the abrupt and absolute repudiation of the transmigration of souls. To twenty-nine men out of a hundred, being told that Buddhists do not believe in the transmigration of souls will be just like being told that Moslems do not believe in the Koran or that Spiritualists do not believe in spiritual communications from the dead. In short, it will be like being told that Calvinists never believe in Calvin or that Communists have a horror of Communism. It amused me to reflect what a vast number of novels of the occult sort were swept into the dustbin by that one swift gesture of the English Buddhist. At least, I fear they are not really swept into the dustbin, or even into the twopence-any-volume box. I fear that the fashionable and popular novelists who write best-sellers about Egyptian princesses reincarnated as English and American heroines will not suffer any serious decline in their sales in consequence of a metaphysical essay printed in a paper in Ceylon. I fear that *Dorinda and Her Dead Selves* will continue to appear on the bookstalls in a lurid cover representing a large idol with green eyes. I fancy that *The Nine Lives of Norma Hellways* will still be adorned with press-notices saying that he who opens the book will open the abyss of abysses. Only for a moment can we indulge in the beautiful and consoling vision in which books of this kind are never written any more, but dissolve into Nirvana and endless night. Dorinda and her dead selves are evidently not dead but only damned; and those acquainted with the character of Norma Hellways will concede that a cat is allowed to have nine lives. But whether or no Norma has nine lives, she is very likely to have nine editions. And whether or no the lady reincarnates herself in an endless series of bodies, the author will doubtless embody himself in an endless series of books. Whether or no the spirit of man can die, the spirit of man's credulity and vulgarity and love of tenth-rate hocus-pocus will not die, at any rate in our time; and whether or no these special spiritual personalities can return, things as mean and morbid and idolatrous and silly will return, until something happens that is not provided for in the transmigration of souls, and trash can no longer triumph over truth.

Anyhow, the English Buddhist in Ceylon has no use for that sort of nonsense. I congratulate him on his repudiation, if I cannot in all respects congratulate him on his substitute. Having given his definite and devastating summary of what Buddhism is not, he goes on to give a most interesting and even important summary of what it is. It is, so far as I can make out, simply a metaphysical meditation along the lines of fundamental scepticism. We are unhappy, it says, because we are continually acting or thinking or feeling on the assumption that something or other is actual and attainable and profitable. But instead of seeking for something, we should rather realize that there is no such thing as anything. Everything that seems to exist is in the very act of ceasing to exist; so that desire is literally another name for disappointment. "Life in its light becomes a never-ceasing passing, a flux, a changing, a thing in its very inner essence passing, never the same for two successive instants of its time . . . in all life, even in the highest sentient life, there is nothing that can be regarded as psychic substance, thing, or soul. This is the central doctrine of the teaching, it is the cardinal point of its enlightenment." The writer is quite clear and courageous on this point; he makes it perfectly plain that

this creed does not say, as many creeds do say, that
material things change but the soul survives them; it
distinctly says that the soul has not an atom more
survival than the material things, and indeed that
there is no soul to survive. It is idle to talk about a
personal identity in a future life, because there is
no personal identity even in this life. Now, I am not
going to develop in this place a philosophical criticism of this philosophy. I merely wish to point out
what the philosophy is, according to one of its most
lucid philosophers. I should like to draw attention
to one or two points in the practical and moral question of consequences. The writer does indeed go on to
maintain that the practical and moral consequences
of this view involve the loftiest practice and the pur-
est morality. But this latter part of his essay is certainly the cloudiest and least convincing part of it.
I willingly believe that any number of Buddhists are
very good men, but I cannot see that the theory
itself, as here so lucidly enunciated, has any particular tendency to make men good.

For instance, the Buddhists call Buddha the Lord
of Compassion; and I think I begin to understand
what those who hold this theory mean by compassion. It seems to me almost the opposite of what
Christians mean by charity. The rough, shorthand
way of putting the difference is that the Christian
pities men because they are dying, and the Buddhist

pities them because they are living. The Christian is sorry for what damages the life of a man; but the Buddhist is sorry for him because he is alive. At any rate, he is sorry for him because he is himself. "The next principle is that Dukka, Suffering or, better, Dissatisfaction, is inherent and involved in life. This, of course, has been already stated in the first of the Four Holy Truths, in which we are not only reminded that the incidents which inevitably wait every living thing, birth, decay, sickness, death, are painful; but that the very conditions of individual existence are fraught with sorrow too." When a Christian saint healed a lame man, he assumed that legs are a legitimate satisfaction. When a Christian hospital cures a sick man, it assumes that life is a potential pleasure. I cannot see, on the argument, why a Buddhist saint or hospital should help a man to anything—except perhaps to Buddhism. And surely the disappointment of all desire is as applicable to benevolent desires as to selfish desires. If Faust can never say, "Oh still delay, thou art so fair," why should he say it any more when he is a philanthropist than when he was a philanderer?

XVIII. ON FUNERAL CUSTOMS.

I HAVE been cheering myself lately with a very bright and pleasant book on the subject of death and burial which appeared some few months ago. It is called *Funeral Customs: Their Origin and Development,* by Bertram S. Puckle, and the point of view of the writer is interesting because in a sense individual. He does not write in the usual supercilious way about superstition, indirectly identifying it with religion. He is rather concerned to show that it is not religion which is responsible for superstition. He quotes the very simple forms actually required by ecclesiastical authorities, and contrasts them with the mass of fussy formalities, old and new, that have been added without any authority at all. To this extent he is undoubtedly quite right. The nightmare pomp which seemed so nonsensical to Dickens, the tall black plumes, the long black streamers, the horrible marionettes of mutes—all that sort of thing was often carried out with religious solemnity, but it had nothing to do with religion. Those forms were never imposed by the Church; they were always imposed by the world. They were signs of worldliness and not of unworldliness; being almost always devoted to proclaiming the pride and pedigree and social rank of the dead man: all the things which religion declares to be obviously useless to him when he is dead. We may agree that it was always a worldly gloom and a worldly solemnity. St. Augustine said it, as he said so many things, a long while ago. He who uttered the *"Pereant qui ante nos, etc.,"* must have provoked many other people to say it. He says somewhere that funeral customs are not tributes to the dead but to the living. But perhaps it is not quite so indefensible to pay tributes to the living. If the demand comes not from the Church but from the world, it may be that the worldly are not always quite just to the world. There is more to be said than Mr. Puckle allows for, even for the boast of heraldry, the pomp of power, altogether apart from the long-drawn anthem swelling the note of praise. On the whole, however, we may well be grateful to a writer who will point out that religion has not complicated human customs, but rather simplified them. I remarked many years ago that the most ritualistic service in the world is a very simple matter, concerned with plain things like fire and water or bread and wine, compared with the existing ritualism observed by butlers and waiters in serving a long dinner.

But why will even the most intelligent people insist on saying that every obvious human custom is a relic of some base and barbaric custom? Here, for instance, the writer suggests that leading the favourite charger of a general behind his hearse is a "survival" of some primitive habit of sacrificing an animal on the grave. This seems to me exactly like saying that taking off our hats to a lady is a survival of having our heads cut off, when we were suitors for a fairy princess. In one sense the connexion is quite correct. Taking off hats is a sign of respect to the lady, in a society where ladies are supposed to be respected. And cutting off heads, in the fairy-tale, was a sign that respect for that particular lady was perhaps almost carried to excess. But there is no reason to suppose that the idea would not have existed in its saner form, even if it had never been carried to excess. Similarly, it is natural to associate the horse with the glory of the warrior; and people were doubtless moved by some such emotion, even if they went so far as to kill the horse to his greater glory. But if nobody had ever thought of killing the horse, thousands of people would still have thought of leading the horse. They would have thought of it because it is a perfectly natural thing to think of. Where a higher type of society thinks chiefly of the dignity and solemn beauty of the occasion, it is the occasion of a procession. Where a lower or wilder type of society thinks chiefly of the doom and terror of the occasion, it is the occasion of a sacrifice. Both are, of course, in one sense feeling the intensity and importance of the occasion. That is why they both do something to celebrate it. But I can never see why we should say that the sane form of it is a variation of the savage form, any more than that the savage form is a variation of the sane form. It seems to me much more true to say that the natural introduction of the horse is sometimes degraded into the unnatural immolation of the horse, than to put it the other way round; and say that the immolation introduces the introduction. The presence of the horse behind the hearse is a normal thing, which has sometimes in the past taken an abnormal form. In other words, this explanation of putting the horse behind the hearse is an excellent example of putting the cart before the horse.

This fallacy, which is not peculiar to this writer, but is indeed rather refreshingly rare in him, is always the result of not using our own imagination: that is, our own inside knowledge of mankind. In other words, it comes from not really believing in the brotherhood of men. For there is no value in a version of the brotherhood of men which does not cover troglodytes and cannibals. People do solemn things because they think the occasion is solemn; and they do dreadful things because they think the occasion is dreadful. But there is no particular sense in saying that they do solemn things merely because they once did dreadful things. There is no need to explain ritual by remote extravagances; because it does not need any explanation. It explains itself. It explains all sorts of other things much better than definitions or abstractions explain them. To scatter flowers on a grave is simply a way in which an ordinary person can express in gesture things that only a very great poet could express in words. I decline to believe that those who do it necessarily believe that the dead man can smell. I doubt whether even those who did it in prehistoric times necessarily thought that the dead man could smell. Strange as it may seem, I do not think they were thinking in that vivid, vicarious fashion about the dead man's feelings. I think they were relieving their own feelings. "Funeral customs) are a tribute not to the dead but to the living," said St. Augustine.

But those who write about primitive man's feelings always seem to start with the assumption that he had no feelings. He did everything that we do for sentimental reasons; but we are always told that he did it for totally different reasons. I have never been able to see the sense of this argument at all. Some men sometimes did dark and diabolical things then; and some men sometimes do dark and diabolical things now. Decadents in Paris attend a Black Mass, which is often a sort of parody of human sacrifice. But if somebody tells me that High Mass at the Madeleine, with Marshal Foch in the front pew, is a *survival* of the Black Mass in the den of the decadents

I shall take the liberty of disbelieving him. It is obviously more reasonable to call the bad thing a relic
of the good one than vice versa. And I do not see
why any number of people should not have conceived the common human notion of having a horse
as the companion of a hero, quite apart from special ideas, which undoubtedly existed on special occasions, of terror and blood-offering and similar
expiation. It is simply a question of the order in
which the ideas occur to the mind; and I see no
reason to suppose that the abnormal always occurs
before the normal, or the inhuman before the human.

I do not profess to be reviewing a book, but only
taking a text for an article; but there are, of course,
any number of things in this sort of book that would
provide texts for any number of articles. For instance, I have never read anything at all adequate
about the very beautiful and profound tradition of
the "soul-cake" or "souling-cake" connected with
the ceremony of All Souls' Eve. The passage about
it in this book is necessarily brief but very compact
and contains some valuable information. It also contains a version which I had not seen of that very
touching appeal in which there is all the tender irony
of the Christian idea. The last two lines are given
here thus:

"If you ain't got a penny, a ha'penny will do,
  If you ain't got a ha'penny, then God bless you."

I have always thought there was something very
moving in that last gesture, admitting the man addressed into the brotherhood of the poor.

Here again it is really a matter of inside information. I mean information which we may obtain merely
by diving inside ourselves. It is doubtless probable
that the "soul-cake" is some sort of substitute for the
funeral baked meats of which Shakespeare speaks.
But it is not to be understood merely by looking it
up in old books, even in Shakespeare. It is to be understood by imagining the moral atmosphere for ourselves. Mr. Puckle has some very sensible remarks
about the effect of War Shrines; and how they silently ended the long protest of two or three centuries against prayers for the dead. But if anybody will
put himself in the position of one praying for the
dead, or, better still, simply pray for them, he will
not have the smallest difficulty in understanding why
the same people at the same time offered prayers for
the dead and gave pennies to the poor. The truth
is that the science of folk-lore has suffered terribly
from oblivion of one fact: that folk-lorists also are
folk. It is not in that sense a science like entomology
or conchology or ornithology. A man must study a
beetle from the outside; because it is quite diffi-

cult to get inside a beetle. Men must be objective about a winkle; they must regard it as an object; some even regard it as an unpleasant object. They cannot all become winkles; but they have all been born men. They ought to have an Inner Light, as the Quakers say, about all the things that men have done, which they cannot expect to have about the social activities of winkles. And a great deal of what is called enlightenment seems largely to consist of extinguishing this inner illumination; or, in other words, sinning against the light.

XIX. ON LEISURE

A GREAT part of the modern muddle arises from confusion and contradiction about the word "leisure." To begin with, of course, it should never be confused for a moment with the word "liberty." An artist has liberty, if he is free to create any image in any material that he chooses. But anyone who will try to create anything out of anything will soon discover that it is not a leisurely occupation. On the other hand, a slave may have many hours of leisure, if the overseer has gone to sleep, or if there is no work for him to do at the moment, but he must be ready to do the work at any moment. The point is not so much that the master owns his toil as that he owns his time. But there are other difficulties and double meanings about the term, as it is used in a society like ours at present. If a man is practically compelled, by a sort of social pressure, to ride in the park in the morning or play golf in the afternoon or go out to grand dinners in the evening or finish up at night clubs at night, we describe all those hours of his day as hours of leisure. But they are not hours of leisure at all, in the other sense; as, for instance, on the fanciful supposition that he would like a little time to himself, that he would like to pursue a quite solitary and even unsociable hobby, that he would like really to idle, or, on a more remote hypothesis, that he would like really to think. Now when modern social philosophers are generalizing about labour and leisure and the greater or less degree of liberty for men and women in the modern world, they necessarily lump all these different meanings of leisure together and bring out a result that is not really representative. The weakness of all statistics is that, even when the numbers are generally right, the names are generally wrong. I mean that if somebody says there are so many Christians in Margate or in Mesopotamia, it is obvious that they are assuming that everybody is agreed on what is meant by a Christian. And we have sometimes seen even Christians who appeared to differ on the point. If somebody says that there is a certain percentage of educated people in Heliopolis, Neb., he will very likely say it as firmly as he would say that there are so many negroes in that Nebraskan seat of culture. Whereas it is rather as if he were saying that there were so many opinionated people, which is a matter of opinion. Even the negro question, now I come to think of it, is considerably less concrete than such severe statisticians make it. There are probably almost as many shades of brown as there are shades of education. Before I went to America, I always thought the expression "coloured people" was as fantastic as a fairy-

tale; it sounded as if some of the people were pea-
cock green and others a rich mauve or magenta. I
supposed that it was either a sort of joke, or else a
sort of semi-ironical euphemism or parody of politeness. But when I went there, I found that it was simply a dull description of fact. These people really
are all colours; at least they are all shades of one colour. There must be many more coloured people
than there are black people. I will not insist on the
delicate parallel between colour and culture. I will
not inquire whether a completely educated person is
a more or less rare and refreshing sight than a completely coal-black negro. I merely point out that
when people talk about "educational statistics" and
make tables of the condition of culture in Nebraska
or anywhere else, there is really nothing in their
statements that is exact except the numbers; and the
numbers must be inexact when there is nothing to
apply them to. The statistician is trying to make a
rigid and unchangeable chain out of elastic links.

All this is obvious enough; but it has been less generally noticed that the same applies to the legal and
economic statements made nowadays about work and
recreation and the rest. In their nature they deal ex-
clusively with the quantity and not at all with the
quality. Least of all has anybody dealt adequately
with the effect of a social system on the quality of
leisure. When we say lightly about a man in some

employment or other, "What holidays does he get?"
we only mean it in the sense of "How many holidays
does he get?" or "How long are his holidays?" We
do not put the question to ourselves in the form,
"What sort of holidays does the general system of
society allow him to get?" I am not arguing at the
moment that anybody is indifferent to the welfare
of any other person in particular; or that any other
persons, past or present, had better holidays or ideal
holidays; all that is connected with very much wider
controversies. I am only pointing out that the structure of society does determine the nature of a man's
leisure, almost as much as the nature of his labour.
And I am pointing out that of all such statistical tables the most misleading may be a time-table.

It is obvious enough that there are men in the
world who seem to labour in a very leisurely way.
It is still more obvious that there are men who seem
to enjoy their leisure in a very laborious way. And
of course it is a very difficult question of psychology
to consider which of them gets the most out of life,
or whether either of them gets as much as there is
to be got. But when people come to making magnificent and sweeping generalizations about history and
progress, when they tell us emphatically that science
declares this and that about the relative wisdom or
welfare of different societies, it is obvious that these
sociological dogmas are very lax and inconclusive in-

deed. We have no exact way of testing the proportion of people in any society who really enjoy its social institutions more than they would enjoy other social institutions, especially if they had been trained with a different social sense. Nobody knows, for instance, whether the noise of modern London is not actually a friction to the nerves, which diminishes pleasure even while it drives people on to more pleasure. It is no answer to say that the people are driven to become yet noisier in order to forget the noise. It is no answer to the question of whether, as a fact, people would be happier if they had less friction, even if they seemed to have less fun. There is no way of measuring happiness in that scientific sense; and the scientists who try to do it do not prove anything, except that they have never had any. Nobody can prove positively, for instance, whether the strategical excitement of organized games is great enough to outweigh the loss of personal self-determination and adventure. A man can only say which of the two he likes best himself; and I have no difficulty at all in saying that. But in modern schools, for instance, what is called playtime has become a sort of extended work-time, though both have probably been turned into rather more pleasant work. But none of it is so pleasant as playing alone to the sort of child who likes playing alone. Some of it is acutely and painfully unpleasant to that sort of child. It is obvious

that sumptuous preparations for playing the latest
professional form of American base-ball are no consolation to one who has a solitary genius for playing
the fiddle or playing the fool. It may even be questioned whether playing tennis is always a substitute for playing truant. Since education permitted
more play, it has perhaps permitted less leisure, and
certainly less liberty.

I think the name of leisure has come to cover three
totally different things. The first is being allowed
to do something. The second is being allowed to
do anything. And the third (and perhaps most rare
and precious) is being allowed to do nothing. Of
the first we have undoubtedly a vast and very probably a most profitable increase in recent social arrangements. Undoubtedly there is much more elaborate equipment and opportunity for golfers to play
golf, for bridge-players to play bridge, for jazzers
to jazz or for motorists to motor. But those who
find themselves in the world where these recreations
are provided will find that the modern world is not
really a universal provider. He will find it made
more and more easy to get some things and impossible
to get others. The second sort of leisure is certainly
not increased, and is on the whole lessened. The sense
of having a certain material in hand, which a man may
mould into *any* form he chooses, this is a sort of pleasure now almost confined to artists. Private property

ought to mean that a man feels about bricks and mortar as an artist feels about clay and marble. It ought to mean that gardening, whether or no it can be landscape-gardening, is as personal as landscape-painting. But this special sentiment can hardly flourish among those who live in public gardens or large hotels. And as for the third form of leisure, the most precious, the most consoling, the most pure and holy, the noble habit of doing nothing at all—that is being neglected in a degree which seems to me to threaten the degeneration of the whole race. It is because artists do not practise, patrons do not patronize, crowds do not assemble to reverently worship the great work of Doing Nothing, that the world has lost its philosophy and even failed to invent a new religion.

XX. ON HOLLAND

I HAVE recently had occasion to visit a country I had never visited before; though it is one of the nearest to us in geography, and quite the nearest in history. I knew nothing about Holland except from pictures, and it was natural that the first impression should be that it had stolen its landscapes from the National Gallery. Perhaps, indeed, the National Gallery ought really to be called the International Gallery. It is odd in these days of the cant of cosmopolitanism, when so many things are called international that will always be national, that we should make such a patriotic claim for a place full of foreign pictures. A collection of Raphaels and Rembrandts is called the National Gallery, while a little shop in a little village is called the International Stores. But it struck me that the fact of the Dutch genius having reached its highest glory in painting does make an important distinction between that country and our own, which is in many ways so similar. Holland has been described by her painters, and England by her poets. This has made the island State yet more insular. The one mode of expression is necessarily more cosmopolitan than the other. Pictures need not be translated. Poems cannot be translated. "The moan of doves in immemorial elms, the murmur of innumerable bees," is perfectly inaudible to anybody who does not know English. But Hobbema's Avenue stands open to all tourists, and is not blocked by a fence against anyone who does not know Dutch or Flemish. The Dutch do indeed improve their advantage by talking half-a-dozen languages very well; but that is never quite the same thing. The duty of patriots is to make comprehensible the love of country; and the difficulty with poets is that they can only talk their native tongue; which is like a secret language of lovers.

I had a very inadequate idea of the grandeur of Holland, which has something of the grandeur of Venice. Amsterdam, indeed, is very like Venice; but I myself, having long improved my mind with sensational fiction of the Opprenheim order, had only vaguely associated it with diamonds and Jews, and persons who murder the Jews to obtain the diamonds. But the traveller walks rather amid the ruins of a great State than the restrictions of a small one. Everywhere is the sort of magnificence that always marks an aristocracy founded on colonies and commerce, which marked Venice in the sixteenth and England in the eightenth century; the private houses like palaces, and the personal genius for portrait-painting. But as Dutch dignity is connected with Dutch decay, an Englishman looks at it with an unquiet mind. It is as though he looked not at things of the past, but of the future.

Of course, when we speak of England falling to the position of Holland, we must allow for those who might fairly talk of England rising to the position of Holland. It is by no means unlikely that Holland is now happier than England. It is quite certain that in a general way the small nations are now happier than the great nations. It may be dull to be a Switzer as compared with being a Frenchman, which has always been in all ages a very exciting occupation. But it is certainly probable that Switzerland is better governed than France; though France is better governed than many of the modern industrial States. Switzerland is better governed because it is easier to govern. It has none of the problems of militarism, of frontiers, of foreign policy, of great traditional controversies about religion and politics. It may or may not be better to be a French citizen than a Swiss citizen; it is certainly safer to be a Swiss peasant than to be a French peasant. The Danes have much more solid prosperity now that they are peasants; though it is possible that they had more international influence and importance when they were pirates.

It is certain that the Dutch had more international influence and importance when they were merchant seamen and colonists, which, in those days especially, sometimes approximated to being pirates. But it is by no means certain that the Dutch have not more comfort and contentment now. This preliminary proviso must be made and admitted before any such criticism. There is a perfectly serious historical and economic case for anybody who says that by far the brightest hope for a great nation now is that by luck or skill it may somehow become a small one.

Nevertheless, nearly every normal person does feel, rightly or wrongly, that he wishes to keep his own great nation great, very much as any man would wish to allow his father to keep the position of a gentleman, however sincerely he himself might have praised the position of a peasant. These things are not easy to analyse, but they are even less easy to ignore. The thing is perhaps most accurately taught in a casual turn of phrase in the old and spirited verses about the British soldier in China.

The Englishman feels that not through *him* shall England come to shame, or even to diminishment. If it be indeed better for his country to fall, the thing shall be done either by a providence that is wiser, or by a posterity that is baser than he. The thing shall come from a heaven above him or from an abyss very much beneath; but not from the man himself in the momentous hour of the fate of his fatherland.

As Victor Hugo said, when his old enemy, Louis Napoleon, surrendered at Sedan, "Any prophet who had foreseen it would have been a traitor."

Perhaps the morality of the thing is simple enough after all; and there move through my mind old phrases, about things of which it may be written that they come, but woe unto them by whom they come! However this may be, most men feel—and certainly I feel—that such an ancient glory should not abdicate. But by the same instinct I felt, with a shiver of realism, that it has lately come nearer and nearer to abdication. Holland only went the way that every great State has gone of which the greatness was purely commercial and colonial; which did not, when the time came, take thought for peasantry and popular religion, and all the more rooted things. Goldsmith, in *The Vicar of Wakefield*, pointed out that the mercantile aristocracies of England and Holland were alike forgetting the populace. England was then in her noon of glory, and Holland in her sunset; and that was a hundred years ago. The mark of this mercantile decline is that it is always gradual and almost unconscious. The Dutch cities contain hotels that were once obviously aristocratic mansions; but our own aristocratic mansions are already being turned into hotels. There are Rembrandts in the National Gallery; but the "Blue Boy" is already in the United States.

I do not believe in a fate that falls on men however they act; but I do believe in a fate that falls on them unless they act. If I treated the matter merely as one of necessity and the nature of things, I should say that England was following her sister States of Venice and Holland. If I had ever talked all the mean materialism about living nations and dying nations, I should say that England was certainly dying. But I do not believe that a nation dies save by suicide. To the very last every problem is a problem of will; and if we will we can be whole. But it involves facing our own failures as well as counting our successes; it means *not* depending entirely on commerce and colonies; it means balancing our mercantile morals with more peasant religion and peasant equality; it means ceasing to be content to rule the sea, and making some sort of effort to return to the land.

XXI. ON BATH

I HAPPEN to have been wandering about in the ancient and modern city of Bath. As it happens, it
is in a rather special sense ancient and modern; it
is not in a visible sense very mediæval. Those cor-
respondents who imagine that I am never happy
except when embracing a gargoyle or enacting the
ceremonial of a guild would picture me as forlorn in
a place so classical; but I am feeling very cheerful,
thank you. Bath is indeed associated with one grand
gargoyle as great as a cathedral. The Wife of Bath
is a figure as formidable as Mrs. Gamp, and conceived in truth with greater charity than that of
Charles Dickens. But, in the main, Bath is, as I have
said, a city of the Romans and of the rationalist eighteenth century, with something of a valley of oblivion
in between. Yet I do not sit down and weep by the
waters of Bath as by the waters of Babylon, or hang
my mediæval harp on an eighteenth-century poplar,
or ask how I am to sing mediæval carols in a strange
land.

The truth is that I, for one, feel a great sympathy
not only for the place, but for the period. I do not
say that I model myself on Beau Nash in every detail of dress and demeanour, but I pick up with great

interest all the stories about him, and all that was typical of his time. And I think the thing most typical of his time was that famous order given by Beau Nash that no swords were to be worn in Bath. It marks a paradox of the time and its relation to our own time. We do not wear swords, but we should like to. Whenever we get a chance of doing it in the Pageant of Putney or the historical procession of the Crusaders of Croydon, we do. Whenever we can do it in private theatricals or a fancy-dress ball we do. And when we can only call up the image of a man with a sword by writing or reading a romance about the eighteenth century, we do. But the real man of the eighteenth century did it and wished he didn't. He was beginning to feel a fool with a lethal weapon dangling round his legs. He felt as if he had an antiquated battle-axe hung round his neck or a battering-ram carried under his arm. Beau Nash expressed the inmost spirit of his time, which worshipped civilization and good sense, when he imposed a policy of disarmament on the city of pleasure.

Exactly the same spirit may be noted in "The Rivals." We write romantic plays and novels about Bath in the eighteenth century, glittering with rapiers and even moderately sprinkled with gore. But Sheridan's play shows a spirit of curious coldness to the romantic side of the duel, and a lively sense of the ridiculous side. The hero fights—or, rather,

is ready to fight—as a matter of dull convention;
but there is no attempt to use the duel to make the
hero more heroic. But, while it is possible to have
a great deal of sympathy with this sanity, it is essential to realize that there was in it something of simplicity. The age of reason was in some ways an age
of innocence. It had more illusions than the ages of
faith.

When Voltaire told man to cultivate his garden,
he did not realize how near the garden was to the
Garden of Eden. I do not deny that Voltaire was
in a sense the serpent in his own Eden. But even he
was in some ways a very innocent snake. I mean that
he saw the whole problem as much simpler than
it has since become—or, rather, than it has since
proved itself to be. Voltaire would certainly have
agreed with Beau Nash that sensible men might very
well leave off wearing swords. But certainly Voltaire, and possibly Beau Nash, would have been considerably puzzled to find that the later period of
dropping rapiers was by no means a period of aban-
doning armaments. The very age in which a man
thought it as crazy to wear a sword as to wave a fire-
brand was, nevertheless, the age in which the world
was most ruthlessly and widely swept with fire and
sword. We do not make ourselves ridiculous by
wearing toy swords at tea-parties; we do not carry
useless weapons on harmless occasions. No indeed;

there is nothing useless about our weapons. Wastes
of carnage and cart-loads of dead attest and advertise
their utility. We kill millions of men with new in-
struments far too horrible to be worn as a part of
evening dress. But I doubt whether Voltaire would
have been relieved to hear that the tortures of the
Inquisition and the poison of the Borgias were being
hurled through the air against whole populations, as
the price we pay for getting rid of a few jewelled
sword-hilts or gilded scabbards. I doubt whether
even Beau Nash would be completely happy in the
reflection that nobody now dreams of wearing a
sword when taking the waters, if it were accompanied
by the reflection that (in the great war) men poi-
soned not only the waters, but even the very air.

What I mean by the innocence of the eighteenth-
century rationalists is the fact that they really had
no notion how short a time their own more rational
mood would last. For it must be remembered that
these new monstrosities really were new; they arose,
if only indirectly, out of the new philosophy. They
were not merely the old tyrannies and superstitions
against which the philosophers had protested. It was
not that the Inquisition managed to survive Voltaire. It was not that the luxury of the Borgias managed to linger in the lighter dandyism of Beau Nash.
It was science, it was the natural philosophy encouraged by the Encyclopædists, which begat Zeppe-

lins and mustard gas. It was the French Revolution that produced the conscription of whole peoples; that produced first Napoleon and then Moltke and then Foch. I do not merely deplore this militant development in the sense that pacifists deplore it. But I do say that Voltaire and his school would deplore it. They would all the more deeply deplore it if they realized that they had done a good deal to produce it. If the scientific satirists of the Inquisition had seen some scenes of the Great War they would have hesitated between the hell they had denounced and the hell they had created.

But war is only one fact that illustrates this interlude of innocence. It felt itself to be more polished than anything that had gone before; but we must realize that in some ways it was more polished than what has come after—just as the smooth stream of the verse of Pope flows, as it were, between two more rugged banks—between the rocks of Browning and the rocks of Donne. Yet it was not, as is often supposed, artificial. There really was a certain youthful freshness about it which cannot be recovered any more than youth. For instance, its scepticism was a form of optimism; while ours is generally a form of pessimism.

These men believed in sweeping superstitious ruins off the green fresh bosom of their mother earth. But they believed she was a mother and not

a stepmother; and they believed that the more
superstitions a philosopher swept away, the greener
and fresher he would find her.

Alas! it was the philosopher who was fresh and
green. But for this very reason where his philosophy
failed as philosophy, it had all the more of a certain
unconscious poetry. It believed it was abolishing
ruins, but in truth it was building ruins; and there
is no ruin so antiquated or so picturesque as that
broken classical column on which was inscribed:
"Deo erexit Voltaire."

That was why, for instance, it called what we call
science by the name of natural philosophy. It lingers
in a certain light and aerial quality in the word
"naturalist," which sounds so much breezier and
brighter than "biologist." It was before science had
begun to meddle with morbid moral questions, making them more morbid than before. It was before
the scientist had begun to vivisect living creatures
or living creeds. It was before he had begun to put
poisons into the body for inoculation and into the
mind for instruction. It was before he had begun
to pose as a martyr and while he was still as cheerful as a saint. We think of the eighteenth-century
naturalist as a big boy with a big butterfly-net; perhaps he was more expert with the butterfly-net than
with the pin and cork. But that is exactly why there
is breeze and bright sunlight in the picture of him,

and why the landscape is the landscape of Gains-
borough or of Greuze. He is out in the meadows,
following a butterfly as he might follow a kite—or
a cloud. He is not cramped and crushed in that tiny
cell that is called the scientific universe.

XXII. ON EGYPTIAN INFLUENCE

WE may reasonably expect that the Egyptian excavations will produce an Egyptian fashion in English drawing-rooms. It cannot, indeed, be hoped that the fashion will pursue all the possibilities of the fancy. Furniture dealers and decorators will surely take a hint from those beautiful bedsteads and tables, that are rounded off with the heads of wild beasts, or rest upon the feet of quadrupeds. I have wondered since childhood why more was not made of the parallel; ever since I could sit on a wooden horse as if it were a chair, or bestride a chair and pretend it was a horse. And it would be pleasant to wave our friends towards a hospitable board that terminated in the tusks or horns of a great glaring elephant or elk. But I fear that the fashion will not go to all its possible limits. It is doubtful if the furniture dealers will deal in mummy-cases for modern corpses, or treat such painted coffins as furniture. It is doubtful if we shall ever see poor Uncle Henry or the late lamented Aunt Mary standing about the drawing-room in an embalmed condition. Such artificial preservation seems to have been natural to the old Egyptians in the moral atmosphere of their own religion, whatever it may have been. For even when we come to know a little of the religion, we know nothing of the atmosphere. But to Christians the practice would seem as creepy as keeping a stuffed grandfather in a glass case. For us, decay itself is more decent; corruption itself is less loathsome than that stiff mask of life; and there is more hope in visible dissolution than in that terrible terrestrial immortality.

But it is probable, as has been said, that the Egyptian fashion will fall short of the Egyptian religion. The society lady may wear the veil of Isis, though perhaps less consistently than the goddess. But I rather doubt whether society gentlemen will assume head-dresses simulating the heads of dogs, in the manner of Anubis; and even whether the ladies will all wish to identify themselves with cats, in honour of Pasht. It is more likely that for a little time the conventions of decoration might be affected and possibly in decorative literature as well as decorative art. The lotus might be substituted for the rose, or even the ibis for the nightingale. But it will be long before any spontaneous Western poet speaks of the ibis as Keats spoke of the nightingale, or of the lotus as Ronsard spoke of the rose. These things are decorative precisely because they are dead; they can be used upon screens and carpets precisely because they have been flattened like dried plants in an album, or microscopic sections on a slide. What the living

Egyptian religion was like, not the most learned man can possibly tell. For we know how wildly the most learned can misunderstand even a living religion. And even our guesses about it have been a great deal vulgarized by the trick of writing trashy tales and theories about reincarnation, which always revolve (I cannot imagine why) round the mystery of ancient Egypt. So far as I know, Egyptian religion did not involve reincarnation. I cannot imagine why romances of reincarnation should always involve Egyptian religion. They also generally involve Egyptian royalty; and those recovering the memory of their former lives seldom fail to remember having been Egyptian princesses, or the lovers of Egyptian princesses. It would seem that, at that stage of the earth's history, all the inhabitants were Egyptians, and all the Egyptians were royal personages. If I have lived before in remote ages, I would much rather have been an ancient Chinaman. I might have been an ancient Chaldean or an ancient Persian. It even seems barely possible that I might have been an ancient European, as I am now a modern European. A great deal of imaginative work might be done for the Etrurian civilization, as Flaubert did it for the Carthaginian civilization. I need hardly add that I do not believe in these Pythagorean notions at all; but, apart from believing in them, I am bored with them. I think I could justify the boredom, if boredom can ever be justified. My mortal life on this planet, thousands of years ago, would only be mystical as my ordinary life now is mystical; and that is quite mystical enough for me. But the memory would be in no sense a vision; it would only be like remembering any day that I happen to have forgotten. The day would be but another glimpse of ordinary daylight; or as ordinary or extraordinary as daylight is today. What makes a real religion mystical, in a much more tremendous sense, is that it claims (truly or falsely) to be hiding a beauty that is more beautiful than any that we know, or perhaps an evil that is more evil. This gives another sort of intensity to common things, suggesting something that is redder than red, or more white than white.

It is possible that the new interest in Egyptian history may save us from the dullness of this Egyptian romance. Perhaps when we know a little more about Egypt we shall not boast of knowing so many Egyptian princesses. We shall be less proud of our previous lives and our pre-natal love affairs. We may make the strange discovery about these dead people that they were living people, and not merely our own dead selves on which we have risen on stepping-stones to our present dizzy height of wisdom and virtue. In short, it is to be hoped that all the sham mysticism that has vulgarized the view of Egypt will give place to the more human thing which we call history. And, indeed, the glimpse we have of that remarkable man who is currently referred to as the "heretic Pharaoh" is a genuine and serious and suggestive piece of history. He is not an empty mummy-case, to be filled with our old selves according to our fancy, but a real historical figure of a recognizable historical type. There is something to be said against the type as well as for it. There is something in it of Marcus Aurelius; something also of Julian the Apostate; something, again, of Joseph of Austria, the brother of Marie Antoinette. Few and fragmentary as are the facts that can be collected about him, far away in such an infinite desert of forgotten antiquity, there are enough of them to converge and convince us of the sort of character involved. He was the sort of idealist who always seeks to simplify; and perhaps has too intellectual an impatience in simplifying. He appealed to that nobler notion of monotheism which really remained in the background of most polytheism, and set up as a substitute and a symbol of God the disk of the sun. It is said that he also tried to introduce a more naturalistic style in art; disregarding the hieratic rules of representation; seeking to make his own image a portrait rather than an idol. I believe it is also true that he was, as humane and high-minded men of his type generally are, an opponent of Imperialism. In looking up some facts for a book upon Palestine, I found he was quite severely criticized for not having taken sufficiently seriously the suzerainty which Egypt was supposed to exercise over the Palestinian tribes. The more Jingo dons and historians flew into quite a wild fury with that withered mummy out of a forgotten world; simply because he was a Little Englander, or, rather, a Little Egypter. All these things, taken together, are enough to make up a real historical character. It is a kind of man who is very much of a hero and sometimes a little of a prig. He often fails in his own fight with popular superstition, because he has not enough sympathy with popular sentiment. It is the paradox of his position that his ideals are impersonal but the interest of him is wholly personal. He will hear of nothing less than saving the whole world and he saves only his own soul.

But these guesses of ours confirm another historical truth of high importance. Such a reformer failed in the old heathen world because of the broad fact about that world—that popular religion was one thing, and personal philosophy quite another. Religion was a social function, almost in the sense that a dance or a dinner is a social function. What was individual was not really religion, but rather speculation. The speculator was separated from social religion, whether he lived alone, like Buddha, or died alone like Socrates. What Christianity did was to combine these two things in a third thing that had never existed before; a public worship that could be believed, and a private conviction that could be shared. It took the popular superstitions very sympathetically; but it grouped them round something that could also be taken seriously. It made a creed that was more than a cult and was also a culture. The more we realize the real history of all that almost prehistoric paganism, the more we shall see that this change was one of the few giant strides made by man.

XXIII. ON ARCHAEOLOGY

THERE is a curious fable that the study of ancient stones has a petrifying effect on people. One of the figures in conventional fiction is the archaeological professor, who is always as dry as a parchment or as rigid as a hieroglyphic. He is one of the most fictitious figures even in fiction. I do not know why it should be supposed that a man who studies mummies must himself be a mummy. We do not insist that the hair of a botanist must be bright green, or that the complexion of every geologist must resemble old red sandstone. We do not expect an ornithologist to hop about flapping his two arms like wings. We do not expect a conchologist to curl up like a creature in a shell. Nor is there any reason why one studying old things should himself be old, or even why one who studies dead things should himself be dying. As a matter of fact, most of the men I have known who had a sort of passion for the past were particularly cheerful and vigorous. Being a practical excavator must mean being a practical adventurer, not ignorant of the toils or even the perils of travel. Scott, in the best of his novels, *The Antiquary*, showed his own shrewdness in making the investigator not only sturdy, but shrewd. Indeed, Mr. Oldbuck is a man of liberal and almost revolutionary sympathies; while his friend Sir Arthur Wardour is distinguished from him by being merely traditional or reactionary. The one old gentleman is an anti-quary, and the other only an antiquity. I do not say that any antiquaries are infallible, any more than Mr. Oldbuck was infallible about Aiken Drum's Lang Ladle. But he was certainly lively and humor-ous, and all the more lively and humorous for hav-ing passed so many of his days among the dead.

For there is here involved a larger matter, which is too little noted. We can see it best if we compare the old romances which the Antiquary studied—or, indeed, the old romance of the Antiquary himself—with a kind of new romance which has been rather typical of our time. I mean the romance about the future—often about the very remote future; and generally at least as strange and spectral as the most remote past. Sometimes it is the description of a Utopia, or perfect state of society into which our so-cial tendencies will evolve. It is not unfair to say that very few Utopian stories have anything that can be called fun in them. The approximate exceptions are More's *Utopia*, and the work of William Morris, with its fine irresponsible title of *News from No-where*. They are exceptions precisely because neither More nor Morris was really modern, and because Morris was rather more mediæval than More. But

most futurist works have not even this amount of
levity; and the reason is not unconnected with the
real case for a study of the past.

We talk of the past as dead; but there is a very
special and definite sense in which the past is always a living thing while the future is a dead thing.
We know that the past has moved on living lines;
but we can only conceive the future as moving on
dead lines—that is, on mechanical lines. If we think
the future calculable at all, we can only calculate it
in a mathematical fashion, by averages and tendencies and consistent curves of change. We can guess the
population will increase in such and such a proportion, or mortality in such and such a degree; but
we cannot think about the marriages or murders of
the future as we do about the marriages and murders of the past. We can guess that this or that in-
vention will be further improved, or this or that
route of travel further developed; that a tax will
increase or a trade expand. Probably we guess
wrong; but certainly we guess in round numbers. We
cannot see the fascinating fractions into which the
real working out of the sum reduces the real number. It is always those vivid fractions—we might
say those vulgar fractions—that we see in the past.
It is the things left over, the things that do not fit,
the things sprawling and struggling, that make the
past so living a thing. That is why every prediction

of the future, even by a genius like Mr. Wells, always looks like a long row of noughts. Our fathers were content to say that the future was x, or the unknown quantity. Our futurists are really content to prove that $x = 0$. The mathematical figure for nought is round and harmonious and symmetrical, and has a fine inevitable curve; but it is also hollow and blank—a face without features. In all these points it resembles the usual Utopian or pessimistic prediction about the human race. But history has not been merely a row of noughts. Religious history, at worst, has been a game of noughts and crosses.

The future is dead, because all futurism must be a sort of fatalism. It cannot foresee the free part of human action; it can only foresee the servile part. It is not a question of whether the prediction is optimistic or pessimistic; it is a question of the nature of prediction itself. The line may go up or down, with the optimist or the pessimist; the line may merely go round and round, with those who believe in recurrence and a wheel of fate. It may be progressive in the pattern of an ascending spiral or self-repeating in the pattern of the swing of a pendulum. But the point about all these patterns is that they must all be mathematical patterns. None of them can be like artistic pictures. The point of all these lines is that they must all be mathematical lines; none of them can be free lines, like the lines of a draughts-

man. It is only in the past that we find the finished
picture; for it is only in the past that we find the free
line. In other words, when we look at what men did,
we are looking at what they freely chose to do. But
when we consider what men will do, we cannot consider what they will choose to do. We can only consider what they must do. Unless it be something they
cannot avoid, it is something we cannot predict. And
so our prediction, whether it is true or not, will only
be dealing with human society on its servile side. In
so far as the next generation is free, it is free to frustrate our prophecy.

Now, the historic past is full of those free actions
and frustrated prophecies. The future can only consist of things expected; it is only the past that
consists of things that were entirely unexpected.
Therefore history, and even archaeology, is intrin-
sically surprising; because it is the study of a story
of surprises. For instance, a man looking at the round
wheels of modern machinery, and delighted to see
the wheels go round, may make a more or less mechanical calculation of what more wheels, or bigger
wheels, or swifter wheels, might be used for doing
in the future. But a man looking at the round arches
of the old Roman and Norman architecture could
not possibly have calculated from them that, a hundred years afterwards, the delicate energy of the
Gothic would be piercing the sky with spires and

pointed arches as if with spears and arrows. That was an act of free imagination and, properly understood, an act of free will. And even if nothing were left of the Gothic but a few grey ruins covered with moss and ivy, even if all the spires were fallen and all the pointed arches broken, the study of them would still be an exciting study: because it would be the study of the intense excitement of an entirely new thing.

We cannot in that sense *predict* an entirely new thing. It would be to expect an unexpected thing. We cannot predict new things, because by hypothesis we can only calculate them logically from old things. We can stand in the present and project its lines further into the future; but we cannot stand in the future and project the new thing really native to the future. We may guess some of the fulfilments of a later generation; but we cannot share in any of its surprises. We may know a little about the heritage of our grandchildren, but nothing about their windfalls or their wilder adventures. If we want windfalls and wild adventures, we must consider the ways of our grandfathers and not our grandchildren. If we want the wildest emotions of novelty and astonishment, we can only find them in mouldering stones and fading tapestries, in the museum of antiquities or the place of tombs.

XXIV. ON MALTREATING WORDS

I READ a phrase in a newspaper the other day, printed in very large letters at the top of a column, which ran as follows: "Crusade to Reform Auction Bridge." And I mused, in a slightly melancholy mood, upon the destiny and the decline of human words; and how clearly the fate of words illustrates the fall of man.

Surely anyone will see something a little strange in that remarkable combination of terms and topics; anyone at least who knows what has been for mankind the meaning of the Crusade, not to speak of the meaning of the Cross. Indeed it is quite equally incongruous whether our sympathies are with the Cross or the Crescent. A Moslem of any historical imagination might well be annoyed at such treatment of the tremendous and heroic trial, through which his own creed and culture passed. And when we consider what the Crusade meant to the men of our own race, the fathers and founders of us all, it will indeed seem a steep and staggering disproportion; when we call up all the imagery which was familiar for so long in all European history and poetry and all the stages of that marvellous story; the first vast movement, anonymous and almost anarchical, moving by mere popular impulse across the world, the mightiest mob in history. For no revolutionary movement of republicans or communists was ever so international as the First Crusade; few were so popular, for it is said that in all that wild democracy there were only nine knights. Then their destruction in the desert and the revenge or recovery, when the despair and darkness opened before the glory of Godfrey's ride; when the toppling battle-towers swayed and sank in flames around the city as Godfrey leapt upon the wall; the high place where he refused the crown of gold under the shadow of the crown of thorns; the return of a deeper darkness, and the last stand under the Horns of Hattin, where the knights died around the True Cross; the rush of the rescuer upon Acre and that vain victory after which the Lion Heart threw his lance to earth and turned his back on Jerusalem, that he might not see what he must not save; the strange and gloomy story of the Fourth Crusade and old Simon de Montfort riding away alone because he would not draw the sword against Christian men; the way in which that golden or crimson thread was woven into the tapestries of every land; whether they showed Douglas hurling the heart of Bruce before him in battle with the Saracens, or old Barbarossa sunken under the river but still waiting with his hand on his barbaric sword, or a light that shone in the desert where St. Louis lay like one dying and mingling the Crucifixion with the Crusade. If we have any sense of the historic influence of these images among men, of how Godfrey blazed among the Nine Worthies or what it was that lingered on the lyre of Tasso, we shall perhaps repeat to ourselves in a curious and meditative voice those simple words, "Crusade to Reform Auction Bridge."

Of course this loss of verbal values comes gradually; and at the beginning may even be a tribute of the lesser thing to the greater. Somebody talks naturally enough about a crusade for liberty or a crusade for knowledge; then the hunt is up and everybody who honestly believes in anything uses the term as a cliché; and we are all made familiar with the rush and hustle of a crusade for vaccination or against vivisection. In fact, the word "crusade" begins by meaning "movement" and ends with meaning merely "proposal," when it does not mean merely "fuss." We receive leaflets about a crusade against waste paper: leaflets that are decidedly waste paper. We receive visitors with a crusade against muzzling dogs: visitors whom we ardently desire to muzzle. Crusades for painting the lamp-posts green or putting the costermongers into livery follow each other with unabated enthusiasm; and we have already a crusade to reform auction bridge, and shall doubtless have another to improve ping-pong. *Dieu le Veult.*

Of course there are a great many other examples in everyday English, which may be represented as every bit as bad. We talk about a man being a martyr to indigestion, without being haunted or shamed by the burning shades of St. Lawrence or St. Sebastian. We say that Pebbleswick-on-Sea is a God-forsaken place, without committing ourselves to the highly heretical dogma that it is really forsaken of God. For it is heresy to suggest that even a successful watering-place can really be an exception, either to the divine omnipresence or to the divine charity and forgiveness. But that single phrase "God-forsaken," in itself so tragic, is also in itself a tragedy. I mean it is a marked example of this tragedy of the gradual weakening of words. For it is in itself a very powerful and even appalling phrase. It is not a piece of sound theology, but it is a piece of vigorous and vivid literature. It reminds us of some great phrase in "Paradise Lost," giving a glimpse of a sort of lurid negation and ruinous quiet; not light, but rather darkness visible. Yet, strange to say, a human being can say this awful thing about Pebbleswick without shuddering. Doubtless there are any number of other examples, which I could think of if I stopped to think. Perhaps there is some touch of such levity even in saying that a thing is "crucial" or in declaring that it is the crux of the question. Perhaps there is a grim reminder of it in the fact that "a Resurrectionist" generally means a body-snatcher and not a believer in the Resurrection.

But my wandering thoughts have strayed rather backwards to the origins of these things than out-wards to the numberless examples of them. I think it obvious that the tendency is a general one, apart from extreme examples; though I would still lift a faint and feeble protest against the reformer of auction bridge being literally elevated to the position of Pontifex Maximus. But though we may reason-ably remonstrate with some very abrupt accelera-tions of the process, it may be that it generally goes on as a slow process; and especially as a sleepy process. Most thoroughly bad processes are slow and sleepy; which is why I have sometimes been found wanting in a full and fanatical faith in evolu-tion. And it seems to me that the moral of all these things is the very opposite of that which is offered to us by many evolutionists. There are indeed many of them so clear-headed as not to confuse strictly scien-tific evolution with a vague notion of ethical exalta-tion or expansion. But others do ask us to accept a sort of general upward tendency; and it seems to me that in these things there is a general downward tendency. In the matter of language, which is the main matter of literature, it is clear that words are perpetually falling below themselves. They are ceasing to say what they mean or to mean what they say; they are always beginning to mean something that is not only quite different, but much less definite and strong. And, in this fall of man's chosen symbols, there may well be a symbol of his own fall. He has a difficulty in ruling his tongue; not only in the sense of the talking organ, but in the sense of the language that he talks. Almost when he is not looking, it is always running wild; or, worse still, running weak.

Now this distinction directly concerns all the talk about new art or experiments in literature. It does not make me believe in these things as a progress; but it does in a sense make me believe in them as a change. I am at once more tolerant of them and less trustful of them. I can see that people must be allowed to play about with human language to a certain extent; because unless it is kept stirring it goes stale. But I do not think a thing is necessarily great because we feel it as fresh; or necessarily small because we feel it as stale. All we are doing, when we pick our words or try our experiments, is resisting the general trend of all style towards staleness. Some traditionalists do go a little too stale. Many get a great deal too fresh, as the landladies were supposed to say. But their mistake is merely in supposing that they have any claim to progress or claim to pride. What they are doing, at the best, is to resist retrogression, the retrogression that simply goes with reppetition. In other words, all artists are dedicated to an eternal struggle against the downward tendency of their own method and medium. For this reason they must sometimes be fresh; but there is no reason why they should not also be modest. There is nothing to brag about, in the mere fact that your only mode of expression is perpetually going to the dogs. The dignity of the artist lies in his duty of keeping awake the sense of wonder in the world. In this long vigil he often has to vary his methods of stimulation; but in this long vigil he is also himself striving against a continual tendency to sleep. There are some to whom this may even seem a sombre version of human existence; but not to me; for I have long believed that the only really happy and hopeful faith is a faith in the Fall of Man.

XXV. ON PLEASURE-SEEKING

THE denunciation of pleasure-seeking is rightly suspect, because it is itself so often the seeking of the
very basest of pleasures. I mean, of course, the pleasure of being pained; I mean, the pleasure of being
shocked, the pleasure of being censorious—in a word,
the pleasure of scandal. But there are criticisms of
modern pleasure-seeking which are not merely the
scandal-mongering of old women, which is a permanent temptation to men as they grow old. There
are criticisms that rest on reasonable and eternal
principles. And one of them, I think, is this—that so
many modern pleasures aim at indiscriminate and incongruous combination. They are colours that kill
each other; they are like the action of a musician
who should try to express his universality by listening to five tunes at once.

For instance, it is not greedy to enjoy a good dinner, any more than it is greedy to enjoy a good
concert. But I do think there is something greedy
about trying to enjoy the dinner and the concert
at the same time. I say trying to enjoy them, for
it is the mark of this sort of complex enjoyment that
it is not enjoyed. The fashion of having very loud
music during meals in restaurants and hotels seems

to me a perfect example of this chaotic attempt to have everything at once and do everything at once. Eating and drinking and talking have gone together by a tradition as old as the world; but the entrance of this fourth factor only spoils the other three. It is an ingenious scheme for combining music to which nobody will listen with conversation that nobody can hear. Recall some of the great conversations of history and literature; imagine some of the great and graceful impromptus, some of the spontaneous epigrams of the wits of the past; and then imagine each of them shouted through the deafening uproar of a brass band. It seems to me an intolerable insult to a musical artist that people should treat his art as an adjunct to a refined gluttony. It seems a yet more subtle insult to the musician that people should require to be fortified with food and drink at intervals, to strengthen them to endure his music. I say nothing of the deeper and darker insult to that other artist, the cook, in the suggestion that men require to be inspired and rallied with drums and trumpets to attack the dangers of his dinner, as if it were a fortress bristling with engines of death. But in any case it is the combination of the two pleasures that is unpleasant. When people are listening to a good concert they do not ostentatiously produce large porkpies and bottles of beer to enable them to get through it somehow. And if they do not bring their meals to their music, why should they bring their music to their meals?

I have noticed many other examples of this kind of luxury in the wrong place. I mean, the elaboration of enjoyments in such a way that they cannot be enjoyed. A little while ago I happened to be dining in the train; and I am very fond of dining in the train—or, indeed, anywhere else. I know that people sometimes write to the papers, or even make scenes in the railway-carriage, complaining of the railway dinner service; but my complaint is quite different —and, indeed, quite contrary. I do not complain of the dinner because it was too bad, but because it was too good. The pleasure of eating in trains is akin to the pleasure of picnics, and should have a character adapted to its abnormal and almost adventurous conditions. This dinner was what is called a good dinner—that is, it was about twice as long as any normal person would want in his own home, and a great deal longer than he would want even in an ordinary restaurant. The train was also what is called a good train—that is, it was a train that swayed wildly from side to side in hurtling through England like a thunderbolt. Nobody who really wanted to enjoy a long and luxurious dinner would dream of sitting down to it under those conditions. Nobody would desire the restaurant tables to be shot round and round the restaurant like a giddy-go-round.

Anybody would see in the abstract that it is foolish to attempt to possess simultaneously the advantage of luxury and leisure with the other advantage of speed. It is merely paying for a luxury and purchasing an inconvenience. Add to this the fact that, though the dinner was long, the time given for it was short. For there were other eager epicures waiting to be flung against windows while balancing asparagus or dissecting sardines. Other happy gourmets were to have the opportunity of spilling their soup and upsetting their coffee on that careering vehicle. Everybody concerned in that trainload of banqueters was in as much of a hurry as the train.

As a fact, these combinations are simply conventions. It is not that anybody, left to his own intelligence, would prefer to enjoy a concert in a restaurant, or a dinner in a railway-carriage. It is that some rather vulgar people do not think a restaurant is conventionally complete without a programme of music, or a dinner without a catalogue of courses. These conventions are in their result quite cold and uncomfortable. They entirely neglect the art of pleasure-seeking, in the only intelligent sense of seeking pleasure where it is to be found. It is generally to be found much more in isolation, in distinction, and even in contrast. There was some Oriental sage or other who said, "If you have two pence, buy with one a loaf and the other a flower." I would myself venture to substitute for the flower a cigar or a glass of wine, only that it would be rather ascetical to consume these things at the price. But I am sure it is a sound principle to have one luxury accompanied by plainer things, like a jewel in a simple setting. This is not identical—indeed, it is inconsistent—with what is commonly called the Simple Life, which generally means a monotonous mediocrity of experience, without either luxury or austerity. The real pleasure-seeking is the combination of luxury and austerity in such a way that the luxury can really be felt. And any sort of crowding together of more or less contradictory pleasures, in contempt of this principle, is not so much pleasure-seeking as pleasure-spoiling. Those who allow the colours of enjoyment thus to kill each other can with strict propriety be called kill-joys.

There is another moral which I have more than once noted, though it is not generally understood. The sort of ceremony that the world complains of as antiquated and artificial is really much more fresh and simple than the ceremonies of the world. The old pageantry of heralds or priests was really more elementary, almost in the sense of elemental, than the pomps and vanities of the modern world; it was more elemental because it dealt more directly with elements. That sort of ritualism might almost be called a rule for keeping ritual simple. Left to itself,

in our secular and social life, it becomes extrava-
gantly complex. The old systems had much more
sense of the necessity of doing one thing at a time.
They had much more of the rational notion of knowing what they were doing.

Thus one of the old Parliaments or Church Councils might have many formalities; but there was
nothing corresponding to the noisy band in the
crowded restaurant. They did not bang drums and
blow bassoons while they argued with their enemies
as the others do while they talk to their friends. An
ecclesiastical ceremony, like the assumption by a
bishop of his mitre and pastoral staff, may seem to
some elaborate or extravagant; but there is nothing
in it comparable to the elaborate and extravagant city
banquet served on an express train. The bishop seldom prides himself on putting on his mitre in a
motor-car travelling at any number of miles an hour.
What is the matter with the modern ceremonies is
that they have not only become elaborate but become
entangled. We have the complication of two complicated things caught and hooked in each other, like
two gigantic clocks wrestling. Moreover, there is the
further complication produced by rapid change combined with rigid discipline. The old customs were
at least old enough to become second nature. But a
fashion is always sufficiently new to be unnatural.
We may think it a meaningless pomposity that a

judge should assume a black cap or a cardinal be presented with a red hat. But the judge does not have to change his cap every season, and there is no necessity for the red hat to be a stylish hat. The combination between the rigidity and the rapidity of fashions leads to a mobilization of an almost military type; and, compared with that, the things that were more old-fashioned were also more free.

XXVI. ON DOMESTIC SERVANTS

Discussions about domestic servants seem always to be marked by a highly modern and enlightened confusion on both sides. On the reforming side we have nothing but the extraordinary notion that you can only improve a family by making it more like a factory. On the conservative side we have very little except rather snobbish sneers at the bare idea of any poor person playing on the piano. The last symbol is significant, because it illustrates the one fundamental mistake of both reformers and conservatives: the notion that the social separation of mistresses and servants must be an old thing, and their association must be a new thing. The truth is that the ancient world was more familiar with its slaves than the modern world with its servants. When Christianity humanized the remains of slavery, the association grew less servile and more domestic; it was only in the industrial time that a new fastidiousness and shyness broke it up. It was an amusing irony. Victorian ladies and gentlemen sniffed over their fierce feudal ancestors whose servants dined below the salt, while their own servants dined below the floor. They would never have dreamed of tolerating a housemaid at the other end of their own table, but kept her in a kind of cavern under the pavement. To do them justice, the housemaid would probably have hated dining with them quite as much as they hated dining with her. A new social spirit had come, and the classes were really separated. But it was not always so, and the very case of the piano is enough to remind us of it. Why, Mr. and Mrs. Samuel Pepys had their servant girl in the drawing-room with them in the evening to sing glees with them at their own piano, or what corresponded to their piano. None of the three had a shadow of the modern embarrassment in the matter; there was no sneering and no snobbishness. Manners were rougher in those days, and Mrs. Pepys might very possibly have clouted the girl over the head; but she would never have been surprised to hear of her playing the piano.

Nevertheless, the worst mistake of all has been made by the reformers, and not the conservatives. For it is a mistake at the very root of all the modern mistakes. It is excellently illustrated in a single fact. It was argued at the inquiry that the chief trouble of servants was in preparing the evening meal for the family, and it was therefore innocently proposed to abolish the evening meal for the family. It was not proposed to abolish anything else, of all the fussy formalities of modern daily life. The servants would still, presumably, have to dust half-a-hundred objectless ornaments that the family never look at, and all sorts of odds and ends of furniture that the family never use. The one thing to be abolished is the one thing that does make the family feel like a family. It is the one thing that does really connect them with their feudal ancestors, and probably their prehistoric ancestors, as well as their most remote descendants—the ancient and immortal institution of the feast after work, of reunion and refreshment in the evening. Obviously, any reformer thinking in terms of reality would start with this as the unalterable reality. Then he would reform other things so as to save it—as, for instance, abolish other duties, give the servant other compensations, simplify conditions so that this might be done without a servant, and so on. Of course, he gets hold of the sow by the wrong ear, and starts making his silk purse of that.

The more I see of the world today the more I am certain that it suffers from a certain tail-foremost trick of thought. It does not so much allow the tail to wag the dog as dock the tail of its dog, instead of docking the dog of its tail. It takes the tail first, and then considers whether a quadruped is a suitable appendage to it. It takes the trivial thing first and tries to put it right, without caring whether it is putting the important thing wrong. And just as a gentleman would not really wish to walk down the street followed only by a fine bushy tail instead of a faithful hound, so it will generally be found that the trivial thing, when separated from the important thing, remains just as trivial when it is put right as if it were left wrong. If a man is so careful of his silk hat, and so afraid of its suffering a spot of rain, that he cuts out the whole of the crown and wears only the brim, he will suffer two inconveniences. First, he may get a cold in his head, which some mystics think more important than his hat; and second, he will also have the needless nuisance of wearing a stiff rim round his head which serves none of the purposes of a hat, though it have something of the appearance of a halo. He will not only have lost a convenience, but also gained an encumbrance. If a man is so much afraid of being thrown out of a hansom cab (as many a time I've been) that as soon as he has got into it he insists on the horse being taken out of it, he will find he has made a double mistake. He has not only lost a horse but he has found a cab—an object which in isolation and immobility is not a very useful trifle to possess or a very easy trifle to dispose of. He has taken away the whole motive force and meaning of a cab; but he still has a cab that is quite meaningless. He has sold a good horse to buy a white elephant. Now that little comedy is constantly being acted in the intellectual world. Men reform a thing by removing the reality from it, and then do not know what to do with the unreality that is left. Thus they would reform religious institutions by removing the religion. They do not seem to see that to take away the creed and leave the servants of the creed is simply to go on paying servants for nothing. To keep the temple without the god is to be hag-ridden with superstitious vigilance about a hollow temple—about a mere shell made of brick or stone. To support the palace and not support the king is simply to pay for an empty palace. Just as such philosophers would deal with the temple and the palace, so some of these other social philosophers would deal with the household or the home. They never think of asking with what object they maintain a house. They are quite ready to maintain the house so long as they can abandon the object. They never seem to reflect that, without that object, or with some other object, there never would have been any house at all. There would have been something else quite unlike a house and possibly more like a hive. This idea of going back to the beginning and considering the end, of thinking of the purpose of anything as a whole, seems to these people to be merely metaphysical and mystical, though it is obviously the only thing that is really material and practical. The course that seems to them practical will leave them loaded with a burden of antiquated shells and ruins. There is a case for using these things and a case for destroying them; but there is no case for the current fashion of preserving them and destroying their use. But reformers of this kind do not seem to care how many elaborate trifles they leave to trouble us, as long as they remove the purpose that once at least seemed to be worth the trouble.

The proposal to abolish the family feast in the evening is an excellent example of all this. There is a case for abolishing the family feast because there is a case for abolishing the family and the family homestead and the family name. There is no inevitable reason why these particular people should live together in one particular house at all; they could be kept in carefully numbered cells in some commodious State prison of the Utopia of the sociologists. But as there are people who like living in families, these are precisely the things that they like about it. They like things of the nature of the evening meal; if they were asked for what they valued the house they would probably think first of the evening meal. As it is, they are asked to give up the social reunion they value most, and still preserve the whole house and all the rest of the housework. The servant girl is still forced to dust the dining-room in which nobody will dine. She is still ordered to polish the dinner-table at which nobody will have dinner. A whole factory of futilities, a vast machinery of meaningless and petty duties will remain to be done, and nothing has been removed except the central social function that was the only excuse for any of them. But the strange part of this modern psychology is that it never thinks of beginning by altering the trivialities. It seems to imagine that French-polishing and vacuum-cleaning are more permanent than eating and drinking. Very few of the Utopian visions offered us today have really removed the small mechanical complexities and conventions of life. They mostly conceive the details of every day very much as they are at this moment in any villa in Surbiton. All that they do alter is the essential institution behind the convention, or the essential idea behind the essential institution. They do not imagine a man and a woman married, but renewing their honeymoon elsewhere than in the suburban villa—in a tent, or at the top of a tree. They are more likely to imagine them still living like married people in the suburban villa, only they are not married. They do not seem so much disposed to imagine some more popular figure than the policeman arresting or punishing people for their crimes, as rather to keep the policeman but abandon the whole idea of crime and punishment, substituting some more humane philosophy of putting all sorts of ordinary people in padded cells till they die. And so, in the case of the domestic dinner-party, they do not seem disposed to save the essentials of it by cutting it down to its essentials; they do not say it should be more simplified from luxury, or more equalized among all classes of society, or given everywhere more opportunity to return to its own original nature. They have no notion of the original nature of a feast, any more than of the original nature of a family. Just as they would alter the eternal family in the fashion of the temporary factory, so they would alter the eternal feast in the fashion of the temporary table reserved at a restaurant. It is queer topsy-turvydom to live in; but it will probably only last our time.

XXVII. ON THE WRITING OF HISTORY

THERE are three ways of writing history. The old Victorian way, in the books of our childhood, was picturesque and largely false. The later and more enlightened habit, adopted by academic authorities, is to think they can go on being false so long as they avoid being picturesque. They think that, so long as a lie is dull, it will sound as if it were true. The third way is to use the picturesque (which is a perfectly natural instinct of man for what is memorable), but to make it a symbol of truth and not a symbol of falsehood. It is to tell the reader what the picturesque incident really meant, instead of leaving it meaningless or giving it a deceptive meaning. It is giving a true picture instead of a false picture; but there is not the shadow of a reason why a picture should not be picturesque.

I will take one familiar example from the first pages of our first history-books. It happens to illustrate all three things especially thoroughly. When as children we read about the Battle of Hastings (possibly even before it began suddenly to be called the Battle of Senlac), most of us who have any imagination remembered one thing about it. Possibly it was the only thing that we did remember. It was the

picturesque detail which says that Taillefer or Tailfer the Jongleur went in front of the Norman Army,
throwing his sword in the air and catching it again,
and singing of the Death of Roland. I was delighted
with that story then; I am delighted with it still.
I did not know that a *jongleur* meant, among other
things, a juggler; and therefore I missed about half
the point of the gentleman's eccentric exercise. I was
very vague about who Roland was; and therefore
I missed the whole meaning of the song and the soul
of the man that sang it. Most of what *was* told me
of the spiritual elements involved, I now know to be
quite false. I was told that there was a great nation
of Saxons, who were very noble because they were
really Germans. I was also told there was another
nation of Normans, who were also very noble because they were not really Frenchmen; they were
Scandinavians, and therefore they also were really
and truly Germans. I was told that a wicked man
called the Pope, for malignant reasons of his own,
supported the Scandinavians who came from France
against the Germans who lived in England. But all
this did not bother me very much, even before I
found out that there is not a word of truth in it.
I had got hold of something; I had seen Tailfer of
the dancing sword; one flash of vigorous vision; one
living gesture of the eleventh century.

Now, the later method of the learned, as adopted,

for instance, in the Cambridge Modern History,
consists simply in leaving Tailfer out of it. It involves merely avoiding any such picturesque things
as swords and jugglers. The early Victorian writer
put in the picturesque detail and gave no explanation of it. The late Victorian writer took out the picturesque detail and gave no substitute for it. What
he did put in was a number of lists and catalogues
and calculations of numbers, all tending to the suggestion that the whole affair had been much more
trivial than tradition suggested. Lists of names, without attributes or allusions, appearing for the first and
the last time in the congested narrative, were the
only indications of human beings. But in so far as
the story had any meaning or moral atmosphere at
all, it was just the same sort of dead and dehuman-
ized falsehood as the war between the Saxons and
Scandinavians. Sometimes it implied that all wars
arose from race; sometimes that they always arose
from money. Sometimes it suggested that William
rode bareheaded before his battle-line because he
thought it would relieve a temporary trade depres-
sion; and that Harold got killed because his sound
Saxon sense told him that getting killed is a good
business proposition. The new histories were quite as
unreliable as the old histories. The only difference
was that the new histories were not only unreliable,
but unreadable.

Now, what I wanted when I was a boy, what I still want now I am a man, is not to be told less about the sword-thrower, but to be told more about him. I ought to have been told all about Tailfer the Jongleur, and in that case I should really have been told a great deal about the eleventh century and the dawn of the Middle Ages. If I had been told anything at all about the song that Tailfer sang, or why he sang it, I should have been really introduced not only to the Battle of Hastings, but to a hundred battles beyond it—to one great battle raging over the whole hemisphere. To know something about the Song of Roland is to know something about Christendom. I should have realized that a great battle in the background, against barbaric and heathen religions, was what gave an indirect dignity to the fighting in all these feudal raids in the foreground. This is why Tailfer wanted, as it were, to bless the Norman battle with the nobler memory of a man who fell fighting for the Cross. So somebody might say to a French *poilu*, "They will tell you it is only a modern diplomatic squabble; but I advise you to forget them and think of Joan of Arc." Similarly the juggler himself would have introduced a whole procession of other living figures. The truth about *jongleurs* would mean the truth about troubadours. The truth about troubadours would mean the truth about Provence and all that fascinat-

ing southern civilization which contributed equally
to the pessimist heresy of the Albigensian and the
optimist orthodoxy of the great St. Francis. The saint
and the heretic both began as troubadours. And it is
in connexion with this last matter that I have just
read one of the few historical studies so made that it
really provides what I want and illustrates what I
mean.

It bears what might seem the rather misleading
title of *The Inquisition.* It has nothing to do with
the Spanish Inquisition, which is what most modern
people mean by the Inquisition. It is a very vivid
and vigorous sketch, by Mr. Hoffman Nickerson,
of the circumstances in which the first idea of an
inquisition arose; and it arose, strangely enough, out
of this same rich romantic land of Troubadours and
Courts of Love. In that rather exaggerated world
there had sprung up a school of philosophers of a
strange and sinister but apparently attractive sort.
They were pessimists, but apparently very persuasive
pessimists. They were highly civilized, and they certainly wanted to destroy civilization. It is no slander
on them to say that they wanted to destroy civilization, for in one sense they admitted that they wanted
to destroy everything. They were not merely in revolt against the Church, but against the universe—
at any rate the material universe. They believed in

the spirit; but they were undoubtedly pledged to destroy the sun and moon as soon as was practicable or convenient.

They held that our whole bodily existence is an evil in itself; that marriage is bad because it produces children; that sin is not so bad so long as it does not produce children. This cheery philosophy spread in the Midi and threatened a secession as formidable as Islam. A Crusade was launched against it like the Crusades against Islam. Out of that military campaign came what we call the Inquisition; it was originally a sort of martial law. Even the martial law was originally rather an improvement on mob-law. Now, to have that tale told clearly and completely, as Mr. Hoffman Nickerson tells it, is simply a clear gain to our culture and comprehension of mankind. He does not excuse the cruelties of the early Crusade, still less of the later Inquisition. But though he does not excuse, he does explain. Even fanatics are fanatical *for* something; they are not lunatics raving about nothing. But in most conventional histories the cruelties are not only without justification, but without motive. The author of this book (which is published by Mr. John Bale), by describing the wild heresy first and its wild persecution afterwards, does make some sense of the story. We can imagine men like ourselves persecuting an

intellectual perversion like pessimism, and wishing
to destroy those who wished to destroy the world.

Meanwhile, there are most romantic revelations
outside controversy. I wonder how many modern
readers have ever heard of the Battle of Muret. I
confess I had never heard of it in my life, though
I knew the rough outline of the Albigensian story.
The Battle of Muret was one of the most extraordinary things that ever happened in the world. A
little band of northern knights, led by the father of
our own Simon de Montfort, surprised and scattered by a single sudden manœuvre a relatively
enormous army of Spaniards and Southern Frenchmen, led by great kings and princes. Mr. Nickerson
narrates it with the topographical clarity of a military history; but he cannot prevent it sounding like
a boy's adventure story. That is what I mean by the
picturesque incident *plus* its significance; as distinct from the old picturesque history which left out
the significance, and the new scientific history which
leaves out both. That is what I meant by saying that
the nursery tale about Tailfer the Jongleur could
have been improved not by our being told less about
the juggler, but by our being told more about him.
The Battle of Muret is more and not less romantic
when we realize that it was a war of philosophies—
a fight between the mystical materialism of the sacra-

mentalist and the disembodied idealism of the pessimist. But merely as a tale it is a marvellously
romantic tale, and it is one of a myriad romantic tales
that are never told.

XXVIII. ON CHRISTMAS

CHRISTMAS unvaryingly brings round the idea of something that is at once special and universal; if only in the form of the ancient human habit of having a universal sentiment at a special time. This ancient human habit, like all ancient human habits, has been the subject of a highly modern fuss; the fuss of men who ask themselves indignantly why they do even the things that they want to do, and even the things that they go on doing. Reformers in recent centuries, having very conspicuously refused to make all men equal, or even all citizens equal, have sometimes raised a rather dismal revolt in favour of making all days equal; as if they were three hundred and sixty-five citizens standing all in a row. The Puritans tried to do it by making all the days as dark as nights; though in a rather different sense from that of making a night of it. The Utilitarians and the industrial civilization they created did literally and not metaphorically, materially and not only morally, make days as dark as nights. They went forward without a single backward glance; driving straight on into the fog; having in the most literal sense no headlights. In the days of their power, they really wanted to sacrifice everything to their routine of rapidity; and if they had found their own transit stopped by their own fog, they would not really have known how to reconsider their whole intellectual position; and they could only have comforted themselves with the thought that, if all days were dull, it showed that all days were equal, and there was less danger of any nonsense about Christmas Day.

But generally the normal people enjoy special occasions without knowing why, just as the learned, lofty, cultivated, enlightened people despise them without knowing why. I do not mean that it is easy for anybody to define exactly why men tend to concentrate pleasure at particular places or times. In a sense it is too practical a piece of psychology to be defined. It is like asking the philosopher to explain, in a mathematical manner, why he feels hungry at breakfast-time and dinner-time, those two great red-letter feasts in the diurnal calendar. A cow goes on eating grass more or less steadily all day; a cow does spread out her meals till they are universal and deal with all hours of the day as if they were equal. Perhaps a cow is more philosophical than a philosopher. Cows drink water, and philosophers, at least real philosophers, drink wine. The very word still used in our magazines for a debate among intellectuals about some interesting topic is simply the name of the drinking-bout or wine-party of the old Greek philosophers. When an editor asks me to take part in a Symposium, I suppose I am really entitled to assume that he has offered me a drink. He has merely addressed to me in Greek (for all editors are learned men) a request equivalent to those mysterious ritual utterances I have heard in the form of "What's yours?" and "Say when." The editor would perhaps be a little surprised if I answered his request with effusive gratitude, naming my particular vanity, like Mr. Stiggins. But the ancient Greek symbol of philosophy is a very philosophical symbol. The wine drunk by the philosopher, as distinct from the water drunk by the cow, does stand for certain ideas of concentration or intensification that are among the sacred marks of man. So the wine is concentrated in the cup, while the water wanders at large through the meadows. And so even the most pagan of pagan philosophers seldom goes on drinking wine all day exactly as the cow goes on eating grass all day. His mind, however exalted, will tend naturally to measure and definition. It will tend also to this idea of concentration in time and place.

Prohibition, like every other form of persecution of the poor by the rich, is comparatively easy to engineer in the plutocratic modern State. For this reason there will soon be, in all probability, a Prohibition issue in this country; and all who have any objection to their country making a fool of herself before all civilization may be asked for their support. But I do not now deal with the matter in the more special and direct fashion, in the ordinary political problem of the pub. For the moment I will only remark that this strange movement certainly will not stop at such trifles as abolishing the wine that gave its name to the symposium of Plato or stultifying Shakespeare by saying that there shall be no more cakes and ale. Prohibition exists to prohibit; and when it is once started it will never stop prohibiting. In a Prohibitionist paper I have just received from the district of Boston, published under the very shadow of the University of Harvard, there is a long list of the things that are to be prohibited next. Smokers will be interested to learn that "wild fear and panic often seizes tobacco-users," and that this weed "gathers earth spirits round those enslaved to it." But this is only the beginning. To say that such things seem to the writer as bad as alcohol is an understatement. "Talk about the drug evil," he cries scornfully, "talk about opium, heroin, and morphine . . . the dope that is sending all America to defeat and destruction i nicotine, caffeine, and theine." I am sure all my American friends will be interested to know exactly what it is that is sending all America (all America, t will be noted) to defeat and destruction. Many must have wondered what it was that had defeated and destroyed them; some may even in their bewilderment, have doubted whether they were really defeated and destroyed. But it is always interesting to know that rout and ruin on that scale can be let loose upon the land by drinking a cup of tea. Personally, I cannot believe that anybody was ever destroyed by an American cup of tea. I have known some travellers who were defeated in endeavouring to get an English one. One of them, a lady I know very well, said on first tasting the beverage in its modified American form, "Well, if that's the sort of tea we sent you, I don't wonder you threw it into Boston Harbour."

But even in the case of tea, it will be noted that where there is tea, there is tea-time. Where it really exists as a beverage that can be drunk, it also exists as an institution that must be observed; and the name of it is not merely tea, but afternoon tea. This element of concentration in time as well as space reappears, as everywhere else in the human story. A certain stage in the slow descent of the sun, a certain line in the mathematical map of heaven that is traced in stars, a certain fine shade between afternoon and evening, is made and marked by the ancient human instinct even for the modern institution of tea. Tea is a libation to the sun in that quarter of heaven, to the gods of that condition of earth and sky, fully as much as Easter eggs are proper to Easter or Christmas puddings to Christmas. It is true that by the necessities of the case it has to vary somewhat with the seasons; and it will be found that the institution takes on a slightly different tone in consequence. In that respect it resembles rather Easter than Christmas, and marks what is, in this merely light and local sense, the practical advantage of Christmas over Easter. Christmas is, quite apart from all its really important elements, the central and supreme example of this idea of concentration and fixity; because it is not a movable feast. Many excessive schools of lunatics have tried in vain to move it, and even to move it away. In spite of all sorts of intellectual irritations and pedantic explaining away, human beings will almost certainly go on observing this winter feast in some fashion. If it is for them only a winter feast, they will be found celebrating it with winter sports. If it is for them only a heathen feast, they will keep it as the heathens do. But the great majority of them will go on observing forms that cannot be so explained; they will keep Christmas Day with Christmas gifts and Christmas benedictions; they will continue to do it; and some day suddenly they will wake up and discover why.

XXIX. ON CAROLS

Every Christmas I ponder again the problem of why old Christmas carols are so good when most modern Christian hymns are so bad. The latter is an excruciating enigma in itself; but perhaps one not to be dealt with except delicately in this place. It is not because our religious *poetry* is necessarily bad. Most of the best poetry in the world was and is still religious poetry; but that does not explain the appalling difference between Marlowe's great description of the red sunset as the blood of Christ streaming in the sky and the actual literary quality of "There is a fountain filled with blood." But Christmas being a season of contentment and charity, I am not concerned with the bad hymn-writers but with the good carol-singers. And it is certain that the early carol-singers almost invariably had, what the more modern hymn-writers emphatically have not, a certain natural carriage and distinction of diction: what we have come to call style.

There is an old carol about St. Stephen, who was (it would appear) an important official at the court of King Herod. I do not give this piece of information as dogma, or part of the deposit of faith, or as absolutely binding upon Christian men; nor indeed do I give it as the result of my own historical re-searches, or as something proved by recent excavations in Palestine or as the very latest result of the Higher Criticism, though some of its results are very much more improbable. I accept the poet's assurance that St. Stephen was a clerk "in King Herode's hall," in a certain spirit which is necessary for the appreciation of this very fine sort of literature.

The first necessity is to have a certain affection for anachronism. It is right in all religious art that times should be telescoped together. Anachronism is only the pedantic word for eternity.

Thus when the carol says that St. Stephen came into Herod's hall with "the boar's head on hand," it conceived that servitor as serving up a complete and comfortable Christmas dinner for King Herod. Some will say that this was rather an early meal of the sort to serve. But the same can be found in any really good modern carol, as in one of Mr. Belloc's, where the innkeeper is represented as refusing the Holy Family in the words:

> "Poor folk, said he, must sleep where they may,
> For the Duke of Jewry comes this way
> With all his train on a Christmas Day."

And I do not doubt that some very learned man at Cambridge has already written to correct this error, and point out that Mr. Belloc is probably unaware that Christmas means the Mass of Christ and was not in general use in the time of the Idumean monarch. I have known very learned men at Cambridge write things quite as funny. But this apparent confusion of periods is as deliberate in the modern carol-writer as it was instinctive in the earlier master of that craft. They really meant that there is a feast of Herod, or of the Duke of Jewry, going on all the time; so that there is in a sense a salutation at Bethlehem going on all the time. He really meant that a king as bad as Herod might have the boar's head carried before him at any Christmas feast. And when St. Stephen is asked whether there "lacketh him food and drink in King Herode's hall," he answered with a certain abruptness which admirably expresses the deep division between the two things that are always contemporary:

> "Lacketh me neither meat nor drink
> In King Herode's hall.
> There is a child in Bethlehem born
> Is better than we all."

There is a sort of logical break, an inconsequence, between the first and the second couplet, which profoundly conveys the fact that the two things are incommensurate. It is not for him a matter of chronological sequence, of the paganism of the Herodian palace coming first and the Christianity of the Christmas feast coming afterwards. It is a question of every man standing like Stephen, conscious that each can co-exist with its counterpart, and even its contrary. When King Herod was represented in the mediæval miracle plays he wore the crown of a mediæval king; and probably wore it sideways like the hat of a music-hall comedian. He was made a buffoon; but he was made a mediæval buffoon; and even a royal mediæval buffoon. Sometimes Caiaphas wore the vestments of a mediæval priest: to suggest that a priest also might miss an eternal opportunity and fail at an eternal crisis. There was nothing antiquarian about these antiquated persons. They did not try to "reconstruct" the costume of an Idumean Prince under the suzerainty of Caesar Augustus. Yet it was not always ignorance: it was sometimes rather a profound and philosophical indifference. They instinctively insisted on the brotherhood of men across the ages. Antiquarians sometimes say that they imagined Herod as being like themselves. It would be truer to say that they imagined themselves as possibly becoming too like Herod.

After the artistic truth that is called anachronism, the next artistic quality is what many would call an innocent incongruity. But it is not incongruity: it is rather a comic congruity. It is the art of the grotesque; but many critics forget that the art of the grotesque is an art. Caricature depends on proportion

as much as classical design. Even much more frivolous forms of the grotesque illustrate this truth. The
Mock Turtle may be a mixture of different animals;
but not a mixture of any animals or all animals. The
Mad Hatter may have a moderately and reasonably
mad hat. But he must not have a hat too mad to be
recognized as a hat at all. Real people may wear
hats of that sort, but unreal people have to be more
reasonable. There must be a shape, a design, and a
relation in fantastic form. Now, although the old
Christmas poets combined many things that sound
profane or preposterous to a smug piety, they always
combined them with the instinct of sound poetry.
There is no proof of this to those who have no sense
of what is meant by sound poetry. It will never be
demonstrated to people who do not know what
poetry is, and it will never need to be demonstrated
to people who do know what it is. But any of the
latter will know what I mean, when I say that there
is instinctive selection in lines like those about the
shepherd:

> "He put his hand under his hood,
> He saw a star as red as blood."

The historical expert will earnestly question whether
a shepherd at Bethlehem would have worn a mediæval hood. The Higher Critic will doubt whether
there is any real historical evidence for the star of

Bethlehem having been bright red. The person who understands these things will simply recognize that he is dealing with a real poet. The poet, I presume, suggested a hood because it was his own habit; and the blood-red light in the dark sky, I imagine, he made up out of his own head. But it was an imaginative head, or he would never have happened to combine the blood-red star with the dark arch or aperture of the hood. It is the same when we come to things counted more incongruous. The legendary gifts of the Three Shepherds are really quite as poetical as the recorded gifts of the Three Kings. But the shepherds' gifts are all the more poetical because they are really the gifts of shepherds. Of course when I say there was a selection, I do not necessarily mean that there was a conscious selection. It is exceedingly difficult to say of any artistic creation whether it was a conscious selection. The writer of the mediæval carol would doubtless have been mildly surprised, if he had read my analysis of his intentions in this essay. But so very probably would Shakespeare have been very much surprised, if he had read the critical explanations of the purpose of his plays; or Botticelli been very much surprised, if he had read the artistic analysis of his pictures. It is one thing to be able to do something and quite another to be able to discuss how it is done. But that does not mean that Shakespeare wrote his

plays by accident, or Botticelli threw his paints anyhow at the canvas. The poet made an instinctive but
imaginative selection, when he introduced that thun-
dering on the closed door of the guilty house of
Macbeth; the painter made an instinctive but imaginative selection, when he introduced a silvery light
filtering through the thin plantation of trees seen
under the shed of Bethlehem. And the carol-writer
made an instinctive but imaginative selection when
he made the shepherd offer his pipe like a toy to the
Holy Child.

Lastly, there is a quality in these mediæval songs
than can only be expressed by the mediæval word
"lusty." There is a grand and even gigantic gusto,
which is never found in modern moral and religious
poetry, or only very seldom and in people of the
same tradition. The good news seems to be not only
really good but really new. It is hailed with a sort
of shout; not with a mere chorus of congratulation,
like a recognized occasion of rejoicing. One of the
carols has for a sort of rowdy refrain the more or
less meaningless halloo of "Ut hoy!" Even in reading it on a printed page after five hundred years,
it is impossible not to have a sort of illusion that we
are hearing the loud but distant hail of some hearty
shepherd far away upon the hills. If it is ever sung,
that chorus can hardly be sung too loud. I will not
attempt to inquire here why the mediæval carol, as

distinct from the modern hymn, could manage to achieve the resounding reality of that shout. I should be inclined to suggest that some part of it may have been due to men really believing that there was something to shout about. But certainly the spirit of Christmas is in these songs more than in any other literature that has since been produced; and if I am forbidden by good taste to express myself in theological terms, I will confine myself to saying in a loud voice, "Ut hoy!"

XXX. ON THE COMIC SPIRIT

Not so long ago the author of what was counted the wittiest of recent comedies produced another comedy, which was received with booing; and even, among those who would hardly descend to booing, received with boredom. As I have never seen either the play called a success or the play called a failure, I am naturally not going to pronounce on the merits of the playwright. But the contrast suggests certain considerations about the position of modern comedy which may do something to solve the riddle. Everybody agrees that the comedies in question are what is called "modern"; which seems to mean that they are comedies about cocktails and artificial complexions and people who walk about in a languid manner, when they are supposed to be taking part in a wild dance of liberty and the joy of life. In the recent case some apparently felt that the appearance of a film hero in blue pyjamas was a little absurd. To some of us, I grieve to say, the appearance of a film hero is always absurd, even when the film has wholly discoloured his sleeping-suit. But even to these too sensitive souls the hero is only felt to be absurd because he is supposed to be heroic. And that involves a truth which may have something to do with the reaction against this comedy. It might be stated by saying that, where there is flippancy, there cannot be irony.

It is obvious on the surface that all fun depends on some sort of solemnity. The Bishop of Rumti-foo is a funny figure because the Bishop of Rome is a serious figure. A horrible thought crosses my mind, at this moment, that perhaps there are some in the new world who know nothing of the Bishop of Rumti-foo and his missionary efforts; who may even look him up in a clerical directory or consult the atlas for the discovery of his diocese. I do not know how many people now read the *Bab Ballads*; but those who do will find many inventions much more amusing than any of the cocktail comedies. To those who have ever known the work, it may possibly re-call the particular figure, if I say that the Bishop of Rumti-foo had another link of association with the Bishop of Rome. His name was Peter. He preached to the cannibals of Rumti-foo and persuaded them to wear clothes; generally to wear his own cast clothes; so that each of those wild barbarians pre-sented the appearance of an imperfectly or hastily attired Anglican bishop. But his most famous exploit was learning to dance; not at all in a languid modern manner, but in a wild and fantastic manner, to amuse the islanders of Rumti-foo. And this alone will serve to illustrate the contrast needed for comedy. It

seemed very funny in the *Bab Ballads* that a bishop
should fling himself about into wild attitudes like an
acrobat; or indeed that a bishop should dance at
all. But I imagine that there were high priests of
old hieratic cults who really did dance at high
solemnities, as David danced before the Ark. Those
people did not think there was anything funny about
a high priest dancing; because a high priest was simply a man who danced. And just as there is no fun
in it when everything is serious, so there is no fun
in it when everything is funny. A man who thinks
the high priests of Rome and Rumti-foo equally absurd and antiquated, will not see any difference between them and the wild priest of the primitive
cult; or between the dancing dervish and the dancing
David. Some regard ecclesiastical emblems, last lum-
ber of an abandoned barbarism, as things to be dis-
missed as grotesque and meaningless. And they
would see very little difference between the insignia
of the Bishop of Rumti-foo and the fetishes or to-
tems of the tribe of savages among whom that excellent missionary discharged his mission. Suppose
that we have really agreed to class clericalism with
cannibalism. It will then be no longer possible to
make fun of a bishop by imagining him clad (or
unclad) like a cannibal. It will be impossible to make
any more comic contrast than we should feel between the ways of the Sandwich Islanders and those

of the Solomon Islanders. There will be no more comedy in the confusion than there would be in the confusion between one set of savages who baked their missionaries and another set of savages who boiled them. Where both are equally grotesque objects, there is no effect of the grotesque. There must be something serious that is respected, even in order that it may be satirized. There may be something amusing in a bishop's gaiters; but only because they are a bishop's. Take somebody who has never heard of a bishop and show him over a huge emporium which sells nothing but gaiters, and it is doubtful whether even the ten-thousandth gaiter which he takes up to gaze at will of itself move him to peals of mirth. Modern comedy seems to be collecting gaiters and to have somehow mislaid the bishop and consequently missed the joke.

Now, when we talk of the artificial and superficial character of the old comedies, we do not mean exactly the same thing. The comedies of Congreve or Sheridan did not, for the moment, take the world seriously. But they did not describe a world in which nobody took anything seriously. The respectable things were there, if only to be treated with disrespect. Moreover, the respectable things were respected things. There were a hundred indications that the things being mocked were things that were generally and normally revered. A dialogue of Congreve

may be flippant, in the sense that he keeps entirely
on the surface. But he does not imply that there is
no solid ground under the surface. The old comedy
is like a scene of people dancing a minuet on a very
polished floor; but it is a polished oak floor. The new
comedy is like a scene of people dancing the Charleston on a sheet of ice—of very thin ice. Both floors
are very smooth; both floors are very slippery; on
both floors undignified accidents occur from time to
time. But we know that the Congreve character will
not sink through the floor; that the earth will not
open and swallow him; that he will not fall with a
crash into the wine-cellar and destroy dozens of fine
old port. In the other case we feel that the whole
thing may dissolve; and there is nothing under that
hard and glittering ice except water; sometimes, I
fear, rather dirty water. But, anyhow, the old scof-
fer was dancing on something solid, even if he was
dancing on his mother's grave. And the quaint old
custom of paying some respect to graves, and even
to mothers, was necessary to the grotesque effect
even of that dance of death. But the comedy of ice
melts very easily into mere colourless water; and the
mockers of everything are really mockers of nothing. Unstable as water, they shall not excel.

For in a world where everything is ridiculous,
nothing can be ridiculed. You cannot unmask a
mask; when it is admittedly as hollow as a mask.

You cannot turn a thing upside down, if there is no theory about when it is right way up. If life is really so formless that you cannot make head or tail of it, you cannot pull its tail; and you certainly cannot make it stand on its head. Now there is a certain degree of frivolity that becomes formlessness. If the comic writer has not, at the back of his mind, either his own theory of life which he thinks right, or somebody else's theory of life which he thinks wrong, or at least some negative notion that somebody is wrong in thinking it wrong, he has really nothing to write about. He attempts to produce a sort of comedy in which everybody is indifferent to everything and to everybody else; but you cannot create excitement by the collision of several different boredoms. Boredom is dangerously infectious; and has a way of spreading across the footlights. The reason is that there is not in the frivolity any touch of the serious, and therefore none of the satiric. The satirist is no longer set down to make fun of a bishop; he is set down all alone in the cold world to make fun of a gaiter. The old æsthetes used to explain that Art is unmoral, rather than immoral. It would be rather truer to say that Art can be immoral, but cannot be unmoral. Unmoral comedy is rapidly ceasing to be comic.

XXXI. ON CHANGES IN TASTE

I AM glad to say that I have to a great extent kept
out of all of those disputes about taste, which are
called arguments about art; though they are not
arguments about anything. The man who said we
cannot dispute about tastes really meant that if we
once began we should never leave off; because there
is no way of settling the dispute. But as a fact, men
for the most part vastly prefer to dispute about taste;
because they do not want their disputes settled. You
cannot prove in black and white the superiority of
blue and green, but you can bang each other about
the head and pretend to prove it in black and blue.
Hence we always find that these illogical disputes
are the most pugnacious and provocative. They produce a prodigious sort of people swaggering and laying down the law. And they lay down the law
because there is no law laid down. There is no dis-
puting about tastes; and therefore there is always
bragging, brawling and rioting about tastes.

I am just old enough to remember as a child
the fashion of sunflowers and peacocks' feathers
made fun of in *Patience* and the old volumes of
Punch. I was born just early enough to hear the
Æsthetes scoffing at what was Early Victorian and

praising what was Early English; crying, as did the lady in the great travesty: "Oh be Early English before it is too late!" I have lived long enough to see the latest school of advanced poets imploring us all to be Early Victorian before it is too late. All the things that the Æsthetes denounced as ugly, all the things which even the Anti-Æsthetes only defended as useful, the new Æsthetes actually recommend as æsthetic. Side-whiskers have sprouted again upon the human visage, to the amazement of gods or angels; and have come back in their commonplace smugness, worthy of their old title of mutton-chop whiskers, to eclipse both the flowing hair of the poet and the flowing moustache of the dragoon. Miss Edith Sitwell in her poetry loves to use the most farfetched and fantastic speech in celebration of the most prim and conventional scenery. The crinoline of our grandmothers, so much derided by their grand-daughters, is almost entirely glorified by this one distinguished and daring grand-daughter. She loves to make a picture in which antiquated hoops and parasols appear to be as natural as gaily coloured flowers and fungi. She delights to dwell on dusty old toys in glass-cases; and much of her subject-matter might be called the romance of Aunt Jemima's Work-Box. I am not now concerned with criticizing or appreciating all this; but merely with remarking on the historical irony of it. While the

journalists go on preaching liberty and licence declaring that up-to-date young people can no longer
be content to be Victorian, the poets and critics are
quietly deciding that nobody who is not Victorian
can now be considered up-to-date. To be Victorian is
to be old-fashioned in morals; to be Victorian is also
to be newfangled in art. For my part, I do not care
whether I am Victorian or newfangled or old-
fashioned or a survival of the Æsthetes of the
'eighties; for all this chronological conflict seems to
me extraordinarily unimportant. But I do find it
amusing to watch the continual rise of new fashions
which is invariably the return of old fashions. I have
not yet seen the Sitwells on lace curtains; but I feel
sure that somewhere the sun is shining and filters
foggily through that filmy veil in splashes probably like yellow soap. I am quite prepared to learn
that horsehair sofas bristle stiffly like black horses
in a striped Persian sunrise. Perhaps we may live to
see a halo of holy wonder round the mug marked
"A Present from Margate" and all the knick-knacks
of the seaside lodging-house. Perhaps we may see
the ever-green aspidistra flourish like the green bay-
tree—or the green carnation.

But anyhow, having lived from the age of artists
who revolted against these things to the age of artists
who revived them, I can congratulate myself on
having kept out of both controversies and nearly all

similar controversy. The things I like arguing about are absolute things: whether a proof is logical or whether a practice is just. I do not want to quarrel with anybody about whether being greenery-yallery in the nineteenth century was worse than being orangery-magenta in the twentieth. Anybody can dress in what clothes he likes or put up what decoration he likes or look at what pictures he likes; and I have never understood why in this department, of all others, there should be so strong an element of pugnacity and even of persecution. I am therefore a pretty impartial critic, as critics go; and neither about the old revolution nor the new revolution have I ever been a very excited revolutionary—or reactionary. But both in the old case and the new, I do notice some curious things about such revolutions; curious in themselves and still more curious in not being normally noticed, by the revolutionaries and reactionaries who are raging against each other.

The first odd thing is that people seem to fight about things very unsuitable for fighting. They make a frightful noise in support of very quiet things. They knock each other about in the name of very fragile things. In the old days, there was always this contrast between Whistler in his cult of Impressionism and Whistler in his cult of Impudence. The method of advertising the art was rowdy and even vulgar; but the art itself was the very reverse of vulgar and was not even particularly vivid. Whistler picking quarrels was an aggressive and self-advertising person; but Whistler painting pictures was a delicate and almost timid person. The coloured canvas of that school was flung out on the breeze defiantly like a banner; but the banner itself was an arrangement in grey and silver. And, curiously enough, we find this contradiction more or less repeated in the provocative artists of our own time. The delicate jimcrack jewellery of the Sitwell school of verse seems the very last material in the world to be hurled like bombs or piked up like barricades. That sort of fancy is fragile in every sense of the word; fragile in the accidental sense of dealing with bright and brittle things, like pictured china or clouded glass; and fragile in the psychological sense, in that it depends on a mood easily lost or missed or misunderstood. Yet its upholders strike the attitudes of aggression and persecution; as if they stood for a definite discovery or a conclusive proof. They certainly exist to contradict the advice given to those who live in glass-houses and continue to throw stones.

Whatever be the explanation of this pugnacity about trifles, even if they be precious trifles, it is accompanied by another practical fact which is hardly sufficiently understood. The innovators of the Whistler period and the innovators of the Sitwell period

have always agreed in using a certain argument;
in which they are curiously illogical even when they
happen to be right. They are content to say, when
their novelties are questioned, that the great works
of the past were similarly questioned when they were
novel. It is surely obvious that this does not go to
show that anything that is novel is also great. All
the lunatics in Hanwell are not great thinkers and
artists, because Swift and Maupassant both went
mad. All the convicts in Dartmoor are not leaders
or founders because Socrates and St. Paul were put
in prison. And all pushing and fussy egotists are
not original and creative men because a few original
creators have been called fussy or egotistical. This
objection to the argument is obvious enough; but
there are other objections which are not so generally noticed. And one of them is that when a Cu-
bist painter today says, "They thought the same of
Whistler," we are entitled to answer, "Yes, and
many thought too much of Whistler though many
also thought too little." It is not true that these new
artists ultimately gain the supreme position their
friends claim for them, still less that which they
claim for themselves; though they do gain more
than would be given them by their enemies. We have
left behind for a long time the conception of Whistler as a Cockney "throwing a pot of paint in the
public's face." But we have also left behind all the

implications of "Why drag in Velasquez?" Whistler is no nearer to being Velasquez now than a sane critic would have seen him then; but the insane critics put him both above and below his merits. It may be remembered with profit by those very new artists who use a very old argument.

XXXII. ON IMPARTIALITY

THERE are many excellent societies, organizing debates as well as dances or concerts, which are careful to explain to their lecturers that they must not talk about politics or religion. What else there really is in the world to talk about, I do not know. But these societies probably do not realize the scope of their own statement. They would be surprised, for instance, if I were to object to one of their concerts at which the proceedings concluded with the National Anthem. Yet obviously if there ever was one self-evident, solid, compact compendium of religion and politics, it is in the four words, "God Save the King." Personally I do not object either to the politics or the religion; on the contrary, I would sing with peculiar fervour the lines which are commonly omitted: "Confound their politics, frustrate their knavish tricks," being prepared, if necessary, to mention a few names by way of illustration from contemporary history and fashionable society. But certainly the refrain in question does consist, first, of a quite definite theological dogma; and, second, of a positive recommendation of a particular political arrangement. It could not be supported by an atheist or a devil-worshipper of any delicacy of conscience;

nor by any practical professional regicide with scruples and fine feelings. These societies generally reply vaguely that it is undenominational religion, or that it is not party politics. But this seems to me very insecure and accidental. There have been groups denominated atheist, and there have been parties avowedly regicide. And I should vastly prefer things thus honestly described and declared; I know there are people who are cowed by the scale of the big stars, or feel themselves helpless in a flood of evolutionary change, and who then say they believe in God in a sense. But I should class them with people who should deliberately go and shoot the King, and then say they were saving the King in a sense, from the work and worry of his royal duties.

Anyhow, an incident of this kind set me reflecting upon what people mean by being impartial; by being undenominational or undogmatic; by being non-political or non-party, or non-controversial. Generally it means something very simple indeed. It means that some people suppose the whole world to be of their denomination; and therefore anything that agrees with them is universal and anything that disagrees with them insane. It means simply that they have never disputed their own dogma, and do not even know that it has ever been disputed. In other words, it simply means that they are very good, sincere, and serious people, only provincial or local or limited in the very last degree. But the curious thing is that this provincial assumption can be found in all sorts of people who are not at all, in the ordinary sense, provincial; for instance, in good classical scholars or good literary critics. I have known several examples in my own experience of this inconsistency appearing in the field of literary criticism; of the very sort of thing that is supposed to be colourless in the controversial sense. I hope it will not appear egotistical to take such examples from experience, merely because they do not depend on hearsay.

For example, some years ago I was asked to write a little book on Victorian literature, for a series edited by good academic authorities. They were very complimentary and courteous, but they thought it their duty to preface the book with a note explaining that they were not responsible for my opinions, with the implication that the opinions were rather wild. As a matter of fact, in so far as the opinions implied were more or less mystical, they belonged to what is by far the commonest, the most cosmopolitan, and the most popular sort of mysticism. Anyhow, they thought it necessary to protect their own impartiality. Many of them were men whom I greatly admire; nor was their action one which I in any way resent. But I confess I was amused some time after in opening a book in the same series called *A History of*

Free Thought, or some such name, by an ordinary academic agnostic. This book was devoted entirely, down to the last detail, to demonstrating the proposition that religion has been a nonsensical nightmare from first to last, that Christianity is dead, and that the world is well rid of it. There was no preliminary note of apology to that. There was no warning against that bias; there was no disavowal of that partisanship. Nor can it be explained by supposing that it referred to the facts and not the theories of the agnostic and myself. I could easily imagine that my information was sometimes incorrect; but it is quite sufficient to save me from supposing that his was always correct. There were no dates in my book, so they could not be put right; but it was afterwards shown that the dates in his book were wildly wrong. No; the simple explanation is that the editors did not think his bias was a bias. They thought that sort of secularism was simply sanity; what has been called the religion of all sensible men. As a matter of fact, there are many more sensible men, many more intelligent and instructed men, in modern Europe agreeing with me than agreeing with them. But they lived in a rather limited world, and within it they acted honestly according to their lights.

Here is another case in my own experience. The excellent popular series called *The Outline of Literature and Art* contains a very complete series of notices of contemporary writers, including one on myself. This, again, is far too complimentary in a literary sense; but the critic is far too sincere to be able to write about my views without attacking them. I might say he is too sincere to contain himself about them, without breaking out into the sort of healthy remonstrance which is controversial rather than critical. I am the last person in the world to complain of this; for it is what I have done with every single author I have ever written about. But here, again, what interests me is that it is not done to everybody. The same review considered all sorts of modern pessimists and atheists merely as artists. The writers did not argue with Thomas Hardy, and try to prove to him that life is not a cockpit of cruelty for the cold laughter of the gods. They did not quarrel with the Shropshire Lad for saying that all our passions are vain, and it is better to be dead. They would not think it necessary to provide an antidote of argument to the poisonous pessimism of *The Island of the Penguins.* For they have a vague idea that all this stale and stagnant scepticism is now the normal air of the world; which shows they are rather ignorant of the world. As I say, I am myself only too delighted that the critic should controvert with me. I should be delighted to controvert with him; and I do not think it would be difficult to defend what he condemns. He complains, for instance, of my saying that natural law

is not inevitable, because the moon is not logically
connected with the tide, any more than the moon
with the moon-struck lover. He thinks this is answered by saying that the first two things always go
together, and the other two only occasionally. But
this is a failure to understand my statement, or what
is meant by a logical connexion. What I said was
that moon and tide do not make one thing in the
sense that two and two make four. And the test, as I
also said, is the imagination. We can imagine the
moon without a tide, or a tide without a moon. We
cannot imagine two and two not making four. In
other words, such a critic really answers himself,
even in saying that the two things always go together. For he admits they are two things, and therefore need not always go together. Four and $2 + 2$
are not two things; they are one thing stated in two
different ways.

What I was pointing out was that natural sequence
is a mysterious thing which is not truly inevitable,
because we could imagine something different; and
that this does not apply to the sequences that really
are inevitable, such as those of logic and mathematics.
I was not maintaining that the repetitions in nature
are not real, or that it is not reasonable to reckon on
them for practical purposes. I was only maintaining
that, as we do not know the reason of the repetition,
it might just as well be a consistent will as an in-

evitable law. All this is an argument on which I should be delighted to dilate elsewhere; indeed, I am thinking of writing a series of articles in answer to some recent critics of my views in general. But I only mention it here as another example of the curious confusion about what is controversial as distinct from critical; and why one man may steal and ride the horse, though it be the horrible nightmare, while another may not look over the hedge and compare it, even in jest, to the hedge of fairyland.

XXXIII. ON AMERICAN MORALS

AMERICA is sometimes offered to us, even by Americans (who ought to know better), as a moral example. There are indeed very real American virtues; but this virtuous attitude is hardly one of them. And if anyone wants to know what a welter of weakness and inconsequence the moral mind of America can sometimes be, he may be advised to look, not so much to the Crime Wave or the Charleston, as to the serious idealistic essays by highbrows and cultured critics, such as one by Miss Avis D. Carlson on "Wanted: a Substitute for Righteousness." By righteousness she means, of course, the narrow New England taboos; but she does not know it. For the inference she draws is that we should recognize frankly that "the standard of abstract right and wrong is moribund." This statement will seem less insane if we consider, somewhat curiously, what the standard of abstract right and wrong seems to mean—at least in her section of the States. It is a glimpse of an incredible world.

She takes the case of a young man brought up "in a home where there was an attempt to make the dogmatic cleavage of right and wrong." And what was the dogmatic cleavage? Ah, what indeed! His elders told him that some things were right and some

wrong; and for some time he accepted this strange
assertion. But when he leaves the home he finds that
"apparently perfectly nice people do the things he
has been taught to think evil." Then follows the
revelation. The flowerlike girl he envelops in a mist
of romantic idealization smokes like an imp from the
lower regions and pets like a movie vamp. The chum
his heart yearns towards cultivates a hip-flask, etc."
And this is what the writer calls a dogmatic cleavage
between right and wrong!

The standard of abstract right and wrong apparently is this. That a girl by smoking a cigarette
makes herself one of the company of the fiends in
hell. That such an action is much the same as that of
a sexual vampire. That a young man who continues
to drink fermented liquor as all his countrymen
drank it, until a few years ago, must necessarily be
entirely "evil" and must deny the very existence of
any difference between right and wrong. That is the
"standard of abstract right and wrong" that is apparently taught in the American home. And it is
perfectly obvious, on the face of it, that it is not a
standard of abstract right and wrong at all. That is
exactly what it is not. That is the very last thing that
any clear-headed person would call it. It is not a
standard; it is not abstract; it has not the vaguest
notion of what is meant by right and wrong. It is a
chaos of social and sentimental accidents and associa-

tions, some of them snobbish, all of them provincial, but, above all, nearly all of them concrete and connected with a materialistic prejudice against particular materials. To have a horror of tobacco is not to have an abstract standard of right; but exactly the opposite. It is to have no standard of right whatever; and to take certain local likes or dislikes as a substitute. We need not be very much surprised if the young man repudiates these meaningless vetoes as soon as he can; but if he thinks he is repudiating morality, he must be almost as muddle-headed as his father. And yet the writer in question calmly proposes that we should abolish all ideas of right and wrong, and abandon the whole human conception of a standard of abstract justice, because a boy in Boston cannot be induced to think that a nice girl is a devil when she smokes a cigarette.

If the rising generation were faced with no worse doubts and difficulties than this, it would not be very difficult to reconcile them to the traditions of truth and justice. But I think the episode worth mentioning, merely because it throws a ray of light on the moral condition of American culture, in the decay of Puritanism. And when next we are told that the idealism of America is to set a "standard" by which England must transform herself, it will be well to remember what is apparently meant by a standard and an ideal; and that the fire of that idealism seems both to begin and end in smoke.

Incidentally, I may say I can bear witness to this queer taboo about tobacco. Of course numberless Americans smoke numberless cigars; a great many others eat cigars, which seems to me a more occult pleasure. But there does exist an extraordinary idea that ethics are involved in some way; and many who smoke really disapprove of smoking. I remember once receiving two American interviewers on the same afternoon; there was a box of cigars in front of me and I offered one to each in turn. Their reaction (as they would probably call it) was very curious to watch. The first journalist stiffened suddenly and silently and declined in a very cold voice. He could not have conveyed more plainly that I had attempted to corrupt an honourable man with a foul and infamous indulgence; as if I were the Old Man of the Mountain offering him the hashish that would turn him into an assassin. The second reaction was even more remarkable. The second journalist first looked doubtful; then looked sly; then seemed to glance about him nervously, as if wondering whether we were alone, and then said with a sort of crestfallen and covert smile: "Well, Mr. Chesterton, I'm afraid I have the habit."

As I also have the habit, and have never been able

to imagine how it could be connected with morality or immorality, I confess that I plunged with him deeply into an immoral life. In the course of our conversation, I found he was otherwise perfectly sane. He was quite intelligent about economics or architecture; but his moral sense seemed to have entirely disappeared. He really thought it was rather wicked to smoke. He had no "standard of abstract right and wrong"; in him it was not merely moribund; it was apparently dead. But anyhow, that is the point and that is the test. Nobody who has an abstract standard of right and wrong can possibly think it wrong to smoke a cigar. But he had a concrete standard of particular cut and dried customs of a particular tribe. Those who say that the Americans are largely descended from the American Indians might certainly make a case out of the suggestion that this mystical horror of material things is largely a barbaric sentiment. The Red Indian is said to have tried and condemned a tomahawk for committing a murder. In this he was certainly the prototype of the white man who curses a bottle because too much of it goes into a man. Prohibition is sometimes praised for its simplicity; on these lines it may be equally condemned for its savagery. But I myself do not say anything so absurd as that Americans are savages; nor do I think that it would matter much even if they were decended from savages. It is culture that counts and not ethnology; and the culture that is concerned here derives indirectly rather from New England than from Old America. Wherever it derives from, however, this is the thing to be noted about it: that it really does not seem to understand what is meant by a standard of right and wrong. It has a vague sentimental notion that certain habits were not suitable to the old log cabin or the old home-town. It has a vague utilitarian notion that certain habits are not directly useful in the new amalgamated stores or the new financial gambling-hell. If his aged mother or his economic master dislikes to see a young man hanging about with a pipe in his mouth, the action becomes a sin; or the nearest that such a moral philosophy can come to the idea of a sin. A man does not chop wood for the log hut by smoking; and a man does not make dividends for the Big Boss by smoking; and therefore a smoke has a smell as of something sinful. Of what the great theologians and moral philosophers have meant by a sin, these people have no more idea than a child drinking milk has of a great toxicologist analysing poisons. It may be to the credit of their virtue to be thus vague about vice. The man who is silly enough to say, when offered a cigarette, "I have no vices," may not always deserve the rapier-thrust of the reply given by the Italian Cardinal, "It is not a vice, or doubtless you would have it." But at least a Cardinal knows it is not a vice; which assists the clarity of his mind. But the lack of clear standards among those who vaguely think of it as a vice may yet be the beginning of much peril and oppression. My two American journalists, between them, may yet succeed in adding the sinfulness of cigars to the other curious things now part of the American Constitution.

I would therefore venture to say to Miss Avis Carlson (whose article in other respects contains much that is very thoughtful and valuable) that the quarrel in question does not arise from the Yankee Puritans having too much morality, but from their having too little. It does not arise from their drawing too hard and fast a line of distinction between right and wrong, but from their line being much too loose and indistinct. They go by associations and not by abstractions. Therefore they class smoking with vamping or a flask in the pocket with a sin in the soul. I hope at least that some of the Fundamentalists will succeed in being a little more fundamental than this. The men of Tennessee are supposed to be very anxious to draw the line between men and monkeys. They are also supposed by some to be rather too anxious to draw the line between black men and white men. May I be allowed to hope that they will succeed in drawing a rather more logical line between bad men and good men? Something of the difference and the difficulty may be seen by comparing the old

Ku Klux Klan with the new Ku Klux Klan. The old secret society may have been justified or not; but it had a definite object: it was directed against somebody. The new secret society seems to have been directed against anybody; often against anybody who drank; in time, for all I know, against anybody who smoked. It is this sort of formless fanaticism that is the great danger of the American temperament; and it is well to insist that if men must persecute, they will be more clear-headed if they persecute for a creed.

XXXIV. ON PROHIBITION

THE Americans are a very self-conscious people. That is the nearest I have ever got to a generalization that really covers that great and mixed multitude. That is the thing that is really common to the optimism of Whitman and the pessimism of Poe; to the humour of Lincoln and the romanticism of Lee; to the Jingoism of President Roosevelt and the Pacifism of President Wilson; to the vulgarity of Billy Sunday and the virtuosity of Henry James. All the characteristics of all these characters had the slight extra touch of emphasis which belongs to a man who is conscious of his part or (in a more favourable phrase) who knows what he is doing. Dickens left behind him a legend of the rudeness of Americans, which is now hardly true enough even to be called legendary. But when an American really is rude, as a cocksure Yankee may sometimes be in a Continental hotel, it is always by overacting his part. It is by being conscious of being Yankee; by being conscious of being cocksure; by being cocksure of being cocksure. But an English tourist in a Continental hotel can not only be rude and stupid; he can be too stupid even to know that he is rude. For the English are a much more unconscious people; much

more blind and automatic and absent-minded. And
as it is with the extreme of American rudeness, so
it is with the extreme of American politeness.
Enough remains even today of the traditions of the
old Southern aristocracy to convince anyone that it
was really the most stately and humane school of
manners in the world. But the Southern gentleman
was a very conscious gentleman; he was not like the
ordinary unconscious English gentleman. I do not
mean that it was a pose maintained with constraint
or difficulty. On the contrary, I mean that it was a
part of him, as poetry is a part of the poet or music
is a part of a musician. But the poet knows he is a
poet; nobody would say that the musician was unconscious of music, or that this type of man was
unconscious of manners. It was not an artificial thing,
but it was an artistic thing. And the American gentleman is in that sense an artist and almost in that
sense an actor. I have met the representatives of old
families in the old cities on the eastern coast of
America who were almost too civilized to be human;
they had no imperfection except perfection. They
really were artists in life; and it must be a terrible
and almost tragic vocation. But there is the same deliberate artistic quality in the commonest and coarsest
smoking-room story told with an ever-lengthening
drawl by an American drummer in the lounge of an
hotel. There is the same self-consciousness in the

photograph of the most absurd business bounder on
the make, who tightens his mouth and swells out his
jaws in the advertisements of a cheap magazine. He
may not be exactly an artist, but he is far from being
an artless character. He may not be a portrait-
painter, but he knows how to be a portrait; and the
photograph of him is not an accidental snapshot.
That sort of art never deals with the unconscious outlying parts of a man, with glimpses of him behind his
back, with qualities betrayed when he is off his
guard, with the automatic actions of an animal walking away. There are more of these sidelights and
subconscious betrayals, both for good and evil, in
the English mode of life. The American always fixes
the world with his face, even if it is a mask in the
sense that he may truly be said to be making a face.
To use a yet more theatrical metaphor, we may say
that he has made up his face, to prove that he has
made up his mind.

There is a great deal of this American psychology
in the contradictions of the Prohibition controversy.
Nobody can be expected to have any respect for Prohibition, but we ought all to have a respect for patriotism. And American patriotism, while very strong,
is a curiously sensitive and self-conscious and sometimes almost morbid thing. The truth about the intelligent American is very simple, but it is not one
that he can always be expected to admit. He is

ashamed of Prohibition, but he is also ashamed of
being ashamed of Prohibition. Even if he would have
preferred the movement never to have come, he does
not like the suggestion that it has come to nothing.
He does not like the idea of so big a thing being a
bathos and an anticlimax. It goes against all his national instincts for that queer process which he calls
"making good." He would prefer that a thing should
make good, even if it is obviously bad. There was
something of the same sensibility in the old days
about the Negro Slave Trade; and there was a time
when everybody's pride was up in arms although (or
because) nobody's conscience was at ease. Of course,
there were people, like Calhoun, who said that slavery was good in itself; and there are people, like
Bryan, who manage to think Prohibition is good in
itself. But I am not talking of these very provincial
prophets of the new Islam, but of the many Americans who are conscious of the attitude of civilization
as a whole towards such new religions. These good
citizens cannot help feeling that the Amendment to
the Constitution is the Constitution, and that the
Constitution is the United States. Such a man has
nailed the flag to the mast, even if he has nailed this
ridiculous rag of nonsense to the flag. For good or
evil, Old Glory has got another star, though all men
say it is only a spot; it has got another stripe, though
the whole world sees it is a stain. I repeat that we

ought all to be able to sympathize with that sensibility in anybody; but in the American it is a very sensitive sensibility. American nationalism is the most self-conscious in the world, just as English nationalism is the most unconscious in the world. It is one of the many points on which the American and the Englishman, so often idiotically identified, are almost comically contrasted. The American never imitates the Englishman in simply taking for granted both his own patriotism and his own superiority. The American is still very insistent in asserting that he has a country, lest the world should still mistake it for a colony. Anyhow, the effect of this on the problem of Prohibition is to perplex it further by turning it into a problem of patriotism. Rather than that Prohibition should dishonour America, America must even honour Prohibition.

I think that this rather subtle and sensitive element in the case must be carefully considered. I suspect that negro slavery lasted much longer than it might have done, being maintained by national pride against the rather cheap challenges of the world outside. Men are touchy about their reputation abroad, even when they are careless about their regulations at home. But Americans as a race are at once unusually touchy and unusually careless. They are quite capable of standing stiffly upon some regulations about New York Harbour, at the very moment when they are sweeping the whole nonsense out of New York State.

The wisest tone we can adopt, I think, is to trust to the revolutionary spirit in the internal politics of the nation, as against any self-conscious rigidity in its international politics. It is an excellent illustration of the most necessary and the most neglected truth in Anglo-American relations. I mean the truth that the Englishman and the American can be friends because they differ, and not because they agree. For the real corrective to the American fad is a purely American freedom. America really is, as one of its greatest men said of his ideal State, a country where the people think lightly of the laws. That easy habit of revolt really is an American quality; it is certainly not an especially English quality. It would be harder to establish so bad a law in England; but I think it would also be harder to disobey it. If, therefore, we congratulate them on the contempt with which a bad law is often treated, our congratulation will be really a compliment. We shall be doing something that we do less often than we should; we shall really be praising others without praising ourselves.

XXXV. ON TOTAL ABSTINENCE

EVERYBODY knows, I hope, the philosophy of that maritime character, celebrated by Mr. Masefield, who had the honour to be the mate of Henry Morgan. Probably the most familiar phrase in it is that excellent one, "But I'm for toleration and for drinking at an inn." The pirate was probably not aware that he was recording the tragic separation of Liberalism and Liberty. It is the tragic irony of the progressive position today that those who talk most about Toleration are exactly those who cannot tolerate the idea of anybody drinking at an inn.

Being myself a Liberal who has wandered away from the other Liberals without ever getting any nearer to the Conservatives or the Socialists, it is probable enough that I shall be left lonely in that lonely inn; or possibly in the sole company of the old, bold mate of Henry Morgan. Certainly if I have to choose between plutocracy and piracy, I prefer the pirates; for that sort of crime necessitated some sort of virtue. The pirate who grew rich on the high seas at least could not be a coward; the pirate who grows rich on the high prices may be that as well as everything else that is unworthy. Besides, the old pirate was continually pursued by the law; the new pirate is not; he is as likely as not to be in Parliament making the law. But there is one thing that I will not pardon in him, if I pardon everything else as the way of the world or the fashion of the time. If I am to tolerate him, I will not tolerate his intolerance. I will not pardon him if he sits in Parliament and makes laws against men drinking at an inn, while he himself continues to sit drinking in a dining-room. There are a good many prosperous and progressive persons of whom this is literally true. Their hypocritical practice is worse even than their inconsequent theory. Even by their own account, they are for toleration, but against anybody drinking wine. But actually, in their own practice, they are for drinking wine and against toleration of it, in anybody except themselves. Compared with that sort of politician, a pirate like Captain Flint, who died roaring for rum in Savannah, is certainly a very honest and reputable figure. And if a pirate may be the object of relative respect to a true Liberal, a smuggler ought surely to commend himself to the most earnest sympathies of the great Liberal Party, with its dislike of tariffs and import duties. The old smugglers were actually called Free Traders; and there are still a good many Free Traders who would be morally much improved by becoming smugglers.

But anyhow, if, as many seem to suppose, there is a prospect of one of the more progressive groups

going to form the next Government, I think it will
be well for all people, of all political opinions, to
prepare themselves to resist some sort of social oppression. And the way to resist these things is not to
wait for the last moment and then shout the latest
catchword, but to go back to the first principle and
be ready for the first attack on it. If there is one thing
I believe in with a solid certainty, it is in discussing
the abstract question before what is called the practical question. In other words, it is clearing up the
matter while it is moral and before it becomes merely
political. What are the real principles governing all
these problems of Prohibtion and True Temperance
and model public-houses and the rest? Most even
of those who know what they think do not know
why they think it. Most even of those who are
right hardly know that they are right and are easily
bullied into being wrong.

Of course there are two totally different questions: whether we think fermented liquor good or
harmless and whether we ought to forbid it to those
who do think it good or harmless. The former is
an opinion; the latter is an oppression; or, to put it
more impartially, a persecution. A teetotaller may
quite consistently think he is right, without thinking
he has a right to take away other people's rights.
Many teetotallers do take this truly Liberal view;
and they are better Liberals even than the mate of

Henry Morgan and myself. For they are granting
a liberty they cannot even enjoy. Still, in preparing
for the Prohibition controversy, it will be better, I
think, to go yet further back and begin by thoroughly
understanding the tradition of fermented liquor itself. Why is this thing so wide and general an institution of human history? only swept away suddenly from time to time in special places, by the
Moslems in the desert and the Middle Westers on
the plains; and even into those plains and deserts
almost always trickling back again; a tradition even
when it is a secret. Has the whole thing any real
relation to the ultimate realities—to religion and the
rights of man and all the roots of our being?

The total abstainer really has a philosophy, conscious or unconscious; it is much the same philosophy
that is now leading some Teutonic philosophers to
run about naked in the woods. It might roughly be
stated thus: something is obviously wrong with mankind; but we believe that the true outline of man
may be reached by simplification. A tree is a total
abstainer; a fish disports himself in the sea without a bathing-suit; and these things are praised by
all the poets as admittedly beautiful and healthy and
complete. Man will now be made complete by shed-
ding, not only the old slaveries of misgovernment,
but the old slaveries of habit; the artificial customs
that have formed like an accretion upon him in the

superstitious past; and the superstitions of special
festivity will pass with the superstitions of special
mortification. Such a philosopher cannot but feel that
wine is a sort of quack medicine with which the
medicine-man has drugged the tribe in a dark age.
Such a philosopher also cannot but feel, when he is
consistent, that trousers are artificial appendages like
wooden legs, or that wearing a hat on the head is a
confession of weakness like wearing a green shade
over one eye.

Such a philosophy is quite coherent and complete;
there is nothing the matter with it except that it is
all nonsense. It is nonsense because it is not natural,
but unnatural: unnatural to man as he is, was, and
always will be. We can say, if we like, that it is
natural to man to be artificial. And the proof of it
is that, while he is both better and worse than the
beasts, when he tries these tricks he comes out worse
and not better. In a race of running naked in the
woods, the hairy animals will always outstrip and
survive him. If he tries to be a vegetarian, the hippo-
potamus will always be a vegetarian on a far vaster
scale than he. The cow will always go on eating
vegetables with a patience and serene continuity
which would bore a man to the point of suicide; for
the cow scarcely stops to sleep and never stops to
think. If he simplifies his life by being a water-
drinker, there will always be much simpler animals

who can drink a great deal more water; and what is even more important, other animals who can drink a great deal less. The camel is not only on the water-wagon; we may say that he is the water-wagon. Man, to whom alone is revealed the divine humility, has everywhere founded his superiorities on his inferiorities. Being an outcast without protection against the cold, he has made himself an artificial skin; and while he was about it, he has made the purple robes of Tyre and the golden copes of Milan. Being unable to sleep under the stars like the stronger creatures, he has huddled ignominiously under a roof; and, incidentally, made the roof a thing like Glastonbury or the Taj Mahal. And having, for some strange reason, broken down in the rhythm by which all the other unconscious creatures live, he has made a rhythm of his own, with special crises and high moments of festival; because the deep mystery of his nature demands variety and the concentration of contentment into conviviality. There he is no more ashamed that ale is artificial than that clothes or cookery are artificial; knowing that without that artificiality would perish all the arts.

XXXVI. ON GOOD KING ARTHUR

ON a recent visit to Cornwall, and following on it,
I had occasion to look a little more closely into a
subject that fascinates me only as it has hundreds of
much wiser men—the history and legend of King
Arthur and the Round Table, including the addi-
tional legend of the Holy Grail. As far as I could
make out, the wisest of them are now inclined to
think that Arthur really was a man even if he was
also a god. And it seems to me that in any case the
god was never so great as the man. A Christian hero
might have the name of a pagan deity; but it is remembered as the hero's name and not as the deity's.
But even about such pagan deities there are points
on which I confess I have never been clear; and,
even where it is obvious that the stories are legends,
it is not always easy to follow the scientific classi-
fication of them as myths. When an ancient Welsh
bard informs me that one of King Arthur's knights
had the accomplishment of drinking up the sea with
several fleets on it, I cannot acquit him of exaggeration. But, if a modern German professor tells me
that this must be a myth of the sun, I am again
doubtful—first, because I am very doubtful about
whether the sun does very often drink up a fleet with

the sea to wash it down; and second, because I cannot get rid of a feeling that men do sometimes tell a tale simply because it is a good yarn, or even because it is a tall story.

I confess I have never been quite able to understand what was meant by saying that such-and-such a popular story *is* a solar myth or a culture myth or something else other than what it appears to be. I am not clear about what is precisely involved in saying, let us say, that the legend of Perseus and Andromeda *is* something concerned with the sun or moon or anything of the kind. Does it mean that all the people who told a story about a hero and a beautiful princess were thinking about the sun and moon, and not about the man and woman? This would seem to indicate an earnestness of astronomical interest, and a preference for serious scientific studies over lighter and more sentimental subjects, which is too rare in our experience of human nature. Does it mean that any people, or even any person, ever said deliberately, "I am now going to talk about the sun and the solar phenomena, and, to make it more clear and unmistakable, I will confine myself to describing a young man with wings on his shoes and a young woman chained to a rock"? Even that mental process is not very easy to imagine; but, even if somebody in the remote beginnings of things did have such a connexion of ideas, it is hardly an exact description of an idea that continued to exist on its own merits long after it was entirely disconnected. We can hardly call a thing a story about the sun if thousands of people continued to see the point of it without even knowing that the sun had anything to do with it. Obviously the story lived by its own strength; it lived solely because it was a good story and not because it was a solar myth; it lived for ages and ages after it had ceased to be a solar myth.

Historically speaking, the point about a popular legend is whatever it was that made it popular. It is that which we are considering when we are considering the thing itself and what it really is. Some natural comparison might conceivably be the origin in the sense of the first suggestion; but clearly it is not the explanation. It does not explain the popular legend for two reasons—first, that it does not explain the popularity; and second, that the popularity is already explained. It is plain *a priori* that no astronomy is needed to account for a romance about a hero and heroine; and it is plain in practical fact that people could enjoy the romance of the hero and heroine without troubling about the astronomy. To say that the story *is* an astronomical story, in the sense of a solar myth, seems to me an almost meaningless form of words. I take the particular solar theory, just as I take the particular Perseus myth, merely as one example out of many. I am well aware that there are almost as many mythological theories as there are myths; and the latest fashion refers rather to allegories of vegetation than allegories of the sun. Indeed, I believe that just now the sun is rather under a cloud. But there is the same difficulty in saying that the hero is the harvest as in saying that he is the sunshine—the difficulty that most people are interested in the hero because he is the hero, or, in other words, because he is heroic. No other explanation is needed; and all other explanations fail to explain. It is certain that it was the heroic idea that held the human heart through the ages; and it is most probable that it was the heroic idea that existed in the human mind from the start. It seems infinitely more likely that the human mind, if it was a human mind, had the vague idea of a hero or divinity at the beginning, and read that idea into certain external events like the sunrise or the springing of the seed. But in any case these material images cannot continue to explain when they have ceased to exist; and we cannot identify with them something that exists without them.

But if this identification is an illusion in the case of common pagan tales like that of Perseus, it is sheer ignorance of history and human experience when applied to vividly Christian visions like that of the Holy Grail. Those who are content with simply saying that the story of the Grail is that of some Cel-

tic talisman, are talking nonsense of the most nonsensical sort. It is perfectly easy for any person of
common sense to state the facts on which everything,
including their own fancy, can really be said to rest.
In all fairy-tales there is an idea of somebody going
to seek for something, whether it be a golden apple
or a hair in a giant's beard. It is not necessary to be
learned or to prove that there is such a story in
Welsh or Cornish or Breton folk-lore; it is natural
to assume that there are hundreds of them. As the
things so sought cover every conceivable variety, it
is probable that some of them are concerned with
something like a cup or platter. As they are all poems
produced by the human soul, it is arguable that all
of them have some remote relation to the thirst for
the ideal in the human soul. The golden apple,
though hardly appetizing, is none the less inspiring;
and the giant, if not exactly a beauty, does in that
sense draw us with a single hair. If there is such a
Celtic fairy-tale about some visionary pot or pan
or other hollow vessel, it is conceivable that somebody at some time did connect this old tale that he
had heard with the legend of the Holy Grail. But
to say that it was ever the same as the Grail, or the
substance of it, or the point of it, is simply to be
unable to see the point of anything. The legend of
the Holy Cup obviously existed for reasons of its
own; and they were the only real reasons. It is quite

obviously concerned with Christian ideas about the sacraments, which counted for much more with everybody concerned than any pagan ideas about any pots and pans. We cannot say that the pagan idea grew into the Christian idea; for by itself it could never have grown into anything of the kind. In short, there is a simple answer to such a suggestion; if anybody says "The Holy Grail was an old Celtic talisman," it is quite sufficient to reply, "An old Celtic talisman was not the Holy Grail."

What is the matter with these modern critics is that they know more about dead things than about living things. They know more about the things in which a few people living in prehistoric Britain may have believed than about the things in which millions of people living all over Europe and America do at this moment believe. If they knew anything about the latter, they would know at a glance what was the real meaning of the real excitement about the Holy Grail. They would know that nobody could ever have been so much excited about the lingering memory of a particular Welsh fairy-tale. But they are doomed to be perpetually finding the small things and missing the big ones, and digging among the dead while denying all the broad daylight that lies upon the land of the living.

XXXVII. ON ARCHITECTURE

WE have all of us been hearing for some time about
the proposal to pull down the City churches. Some
of us have a certain sympathy with the view that it
would be much better to pull down the City. In the
long reaches of history the irony of the contrast dis-
appears. There must be a good many Greek or
Egyptian temples still standing when the towns or
villages that clustered about them have dissolved
into dust. In looking at those temples we still have,
if we are at all imaginative, a sort of mystical sympathy. We have a sense that, after all, the temple
did not really exist to serve the city, but to serve
the god. But it is a sort of sympathy we seem only
able to feel in the case of a heathen god. Any number of neo-pagan poems have been written describing such gods as still hovering like ghosts over such
temples. Any number of modern poets have written
about ancient ruins still haunted by dog-headed
Anubis or great green-eyed Pasht. They seldom expressed much sympathy for the human inhabitants
of those vanished cities. But, in the case of the vanished cities, at least the inhabitants did inhabit. They
worked, wedded, dined, and slept in their own town,
and were often attached to it by a high religion of

patriotism. So did the inhabitants of our City, in the days when people built churches there. Now that the City has become a vast warehouse, there is much less cause for a poetic lament over its destruction. The reader will be relieved to hear, however, that I have no immediate intention of setting fire to London, or of attempting to repeat the great conflagration which was recorded (entirely wrong) on the Monument. I merely say, in a general historical sense, that the mysterious description of a man as being Something in the City might have been extended in ancient times even to so humble a calling as being a Priest in the City. And I do say that, when we see humanity in retrospect and perspective, we generally find their religion more interesting than their commerce. Even the most commercial cities of antiquity, like Tyre and Carthage, were not so lively and entertaining when they were making out bills-of-lading or recording the fluctuation of the shekel as compared with the drachma, as when the more poetic side of their nature led them to throw babies into the furnace of Moloch.

But the comparison of commercial and religious centres is connected with another question that is perhaps more immediately modern than the worship of Moloch. We have not got quite so far as reviving that sort of Eastern mysticism as yet, though there is no saying what we may come to eventually, with a

judicious combination of neo-pagan nature-worship
and our efforts to restrict the population. But, anyhow, it is more and more plain that commerce is cosmopolitan, while religion is generally to some extent
national, even if it is also international. Being an expression of the whole life of a people, it gives some
expression to the local and traditional life; whereas
mere commercialism of its nature becomes more and
more a shuffling and interchange of different products. The London churches do preserve a certain
historic character of London; they do remind us of
a typical passage in the history of England. But the
merely commercial life of England becomes less and
less English; and the material machinery of London is looking more and more like New York. It
seems likely that, as has so often happened, things
native and domestic will have to retire into sanc-
tuary. It will be a long time at least before the last
monument of Wren vanishes with the fall of St.
Paul's Cathedral, as the last monument of the Regent has vanished with the fall of Regent Street.

In that sense it is not so much a question of the
preservation of London churches as of the preservation of London. London has a soul of its own; it
therefore has a soul to be saved; but nobody seems
to bother very much about saving it. And it seems
possible that the quaint old Wren churches might
still do something towards saving the soul of Lon-

don, even if we have given up all hope of any churches saving the souls of Londoners. For those seventeenth-century buildings had a character and expressed a spirit, even if it be not what I myself should regard as the highest spirit. I am (as my enemies have discovered with diabolical, but slightly monotonous, glee) a mediævalist; and it is my instinct to seek the highest spirit in what was once the highest spire. For the old Gothic St. Paul's, that stood on Ludgate Hill before the Great Fire, was said to be the loftiest building in Christendom. It must have looked very magnificent, rising to such a height upon such a hill. Old St. Paul's might even have been spared by the American invader as being quite a respectable sky-scraper.

Nevertheless, I do not desire the present Renaissance dome of St. Paul's to be immediately replaced by a Woolworth tower. However it may stand in relation to Christendom, it stands in a very important position in relation to Europe. It does to that extent represent the spirit of Europe; and in this particular conflict I sympathize with the spirit of Europe as against the spirit of America. Something of the same part is played in a smaller way by the other Renaissance churches; in so far as they do testify to the idea that culture is a thing rather of quality than quantity. They do suggest that quaint things in quiet places may reveal the secret of our deep human past often better than buildings that take up much more room in the streets, and also much more room in the newspapers. They do stand, in some fashion, for the moment, for the fact that it is not the sky-scraper that is nearest to the sky. A man must have some little sense of craftsmanship and history to know how good is some of the seventeenth-century carving, even of the florid and lightly classical sort. He does not need anything but a neck to crane and eyes to goggle with in order to appreciate a sky-scraper. The taste for mere size is not merely more vulgar; it is also more backward and barbaric. It is all the difference between Rembrandt or Velasquez studying the subtleties of an ordinary face and the yokels in a village staring at the giant in a show. And, in so far as it is a war between barbarism and civilization, I hope I am on the side of civilization not for the first time.

But even where the larger thing is all right in its place, it is here out of place. Even when it is good as a sky-scraper, it is not suited to the sky. The first rule of all good scene-painting is to remember the back-scene. It is an error to paint even Aladdin's Palace without knowing whether its domes and minarets are to be outlined against the back-scene of the Blasted Heath or of the Nile with the barge of Cleopatra. The more inappropriate is the background, the more it will fall forward into the foreground. And our scenery, in several senses, has rather a way of falling down on the actors. Our scenery is of the sort that keeps the scene-shifter very busy shifting. Our back-scene is always a transformation scene. To some it may seem a rather dismal sort of dissolving view. To others (including myself) its cold clouds and gradations of grey seem to be the very vision of real romance. But, anyhow, English weather is emphatically weather; as is implied when we talk of having to weather it. There is no such thing as the English climate. Now the best American architecture is very fine architecture, as, for example, the Pennsylvania Railway Station in New York. But the best American architecture is classical architecture, of the same kind as the best Greek and Roman architecture. At least, it is partly of the same kind, and partly for the same reason. It was built for a climate; it was built to stand up clear and clean-cut against a sky that looks as solid and steady as the stone; a pure pattern of white upon blue. It is suitable to the hard light and the cloudless spaces about the towers of Manhattan; and there, like anything else that is in its place, it is a splendid thing to see. But even the invaders who have brought over American buildings have not yet imported any large blue fragments of American sky.

XXXVIII. ON SHAKESPEARE

I HAVE recently read with very great interest a book
on what is not perhaps entirely a new subject. I refer to the subject of Shakespeare; not without refer-
ence to the subject of Shakespeare's Sonnets, of the
Dark Lady and the poet's relation to Southampton
and Essex and Bacon and various eminent men of his
time. The book is by the Comtesse de Chambrun and
is published by Appleton; and it seems to me both
fascinating and convincing. I hasten to say that the
lady is very learned and I am very ignorant. I do
not profess to know much about Shakespeare, outside
such superfluous trifling as the reading of his literary
works. Madame de Chambrun's book is called *Shakespeare, Actor-Poet*; and I must humbly confess that
I have known him only in his humbler capacity as a
poet, and have never devoted myself to the more
exhausting occupation of studying all the green-room
gossip about him as an actor. But it is very right that
more scholarly people should study the biographi-
cal problem; and even a poor literary critic may
be allowed to judge their studies as literature. And
this study seems to me to be one very valuable to
literature; and not, like so many of the Baconian
penny-dreadfuls, a mere insult to literature. Indeed

some Baconian books are quite as much of an insult
to Bacon as to Shakespeare. I have no authority
to decide the controversies of fact raised here, about
the relation of Southampton to the Sonnets or the
discovery of the Dark Lady in the family of Davenant. I can only say that to a plain man the arguments seem at least to be of a plain sort. Thus, I
have never had any reason to quarrel with Mr.
Frank Harris or Mr. Bernard Shaw about the claims
of Miss Mary Fitton, or to break a lance for or
against that questionable queen of beauty. I have
lances enough to break with them about more important things. But to my simplicity it does seem
rather notable that next to nothing is known about
the Dark Lady except that she was dark; and that
precious little seems to be known about Mary Fitton
except that she was fair. Or again, I profess myself
utterly incompetent to consider the question of
what "T. T." meant by "W. H."; and I do not
think the difficulty will interfere very much with my
joy in saying to myself, "But thine immortal beauty
shall not fade," or, "Give not a windy night a rainy
morrow." But if it be true, as it is here stated, that
some of these sonnets were already written when
William Herbert, Lord Pembroke, was only eleven
years old, he certainly must have been a precocious
child if what Shakespeare says about him is at all
appropriate. There may be ingenious answers to these

things that I do not know. But to guileless ignorance like my own the point seems rather a practical
one. As a matter of fact, I have generally found
in these cases that the ingenious explanations were
a little too ingenious. But, as I have said, I have no
intention of dogmatizing on these problems. Madame de Chambrun's theory is that the young man
for whom Shakespeare had such a hero-worship was
his own patron and protector, the Earl of Southampton; for whom indeed she has some little hero-
worship herself. But she gives very good and
convincing grounds for regarding him as something
of a hero. I am pretty sure she is quite right in saying that the rebellion of Essex and Southampton
was essentially just and public-spirited. She says
that if it had succeeded they would have been
handed down to all history as patriots and reformers. I am also quite sure she is right in saying that
it was rather a rebellion against Cecil than against
Elizabeth; that alone would make it creditable. It
is curious to note that, in this account, Bacon and
Shakespeare, so far from being conspirators and col-
laborators, were two antagonistic figures in two opposite factions; one on each side of a serious civil
war. Bacon was the bitter accuser of Essex; indeed,
Bacon had probably become a sort of hack and servant of Cecil. Shakespeare was of course a friend and
follower of Southampton, who was a friend and

follower of Essex. According to this account, Shakespeare was presenting plays like "Richard II" as deliberate political demonstrations, designed to warn weak sovereigns of the need of greater wisdom, at the very time when Bacon was drawing up the heads of his detailed and virulent denunciation of the rebel. However this may be, it is practically certain that there was the chasm between the two great men, whom some have blended into one great man (we might say into one great monster). This theory would make an even stranger monster of the Baconian version of Bacon. Not only was he capable of leading two separate public lives, but even of figuring in two opposite political parties. He must have been plotting against himself all night and condemning himself to be hanged on the following day.

If I say that this fancy would turn Bacon and Shakespeare into Jekyll and Hyde, the partisans of the two parties will probably dispute rather eagerly about which was which. But I for one have very little doubt on that point. And I am glad to find that Madame de Chambrun thinks very much the same and knows very much more. If ever there was a base business in human history, it was the method of government which Burleigh and his son conducted in England in the name of Elizabeth; and, I am sorry to say, to some extent with the assistance of Bacon. The people whom Robert Cecil destroyed

were all more honest than himself (not that that
was saying much) and some of them were sufficiently
honourable and spirited to dwarf his little hunch-
backed figure even by their dignity in the hour of
death. Whether it were Essex or Mary Stuart or
even poor Guy Fawkes, they might have stood on
the scaffold only in order to make him look small.
And I am heartily glad to hear it, if it be true, that
this nest of nasty plutocrats, with Cecil in the midst
of it, counted among its enemies the greatest of
Englishmen. It gives me great pleasure to think
that it was of those Tudor politicians that he was
thinking, when he talked of strength by limping
away disabled, and art made tongue-tied by authority and captive good attending captain ill. The
last line must have described a good many scenes
on the scaffold in the sixteenth century. It may be
difficult to imagine Shakespeare greater than Shakespeare. But it is possible that if his friends had tri-
umphed and his cause and faith revived, he might
in some unthinkable transfiguration have been
greater than himself.

I know much less of the other problem involved,
which is entirely one of private life and not of public policy. I mean the question of that mysterious
and sinister woman towards whom the sonneteer re-
vives the ancient rage of inconsistencies; the *odi et
amo* of Catullus. But even I, as a mere casual reader

of things in general, had certainly heard of the joke or scandal which is said to have suggested Sir William Davenant was a natural son of William Shakespeare. Whether this was so or not, Shakespeare certainly knew the Davenants, who kept an inn where he visited and where (as the writer of this book explains) Southampton himself appeared on the scene at a later stage. Her theory is that Mrs. Davenant was what we should now call a vamp; that she had at one time vamped the poet and went on later to vamp the peer. But the poet, though his feelings were mixed, could already see through the lady, and was furious at the duping of his friend; and out of this triple tangle of passions came the great tragic sequence of the Sonnets. Upon this I cannot pronounce, beyond repeating that it is set out in this book with great cogency, comprehension, and grip; and without a trace of that indefinable disproportion and lack of balance, which makes many learned and ingenious works on such subjects smell faintly of the madhouse. The writer keeps control of the subject; we feel that, though her conclusions are definite, she would not be seriously upset if they were definitely disproved. She appeals to facts and fairness throughout; and nobody can do more. The documentation and system of references seems to be very thorough; and, in a matter which I am better able to judge, there is nowhere that sense of strain in the argument, or of something altogether far-fetched in the explanation, which continually jars us in most reconstructions of this kind, especially in the dangerous era of Elizabeth. Perhaps after all, that era really was the great spiritual battle; and Shakespeare and Bacon really were the spirits that met in conflict. But anyhow, it is a queer paradox that Shakespeare was an obscure and almost unhistorical figure; according to some nameless or worthless, according to others impersonal and self-effacing; but anyhow somewhat elusive and secret; and from him came a cataract of clear song and natural eloquence; while Bacon was a public man of wide renown and national scientific philosophy; and out of him have come riddles and oracles and fantastic cryptograms and a lifelong hobby for lunatics.

XXXIX. ON EDWIN DROOD

Ever since the real tragedy of the premature death of Dickens interrupted the fictitious tragedy of the premature death of Drood, there has been a continuous series of suggestions for the conclusion of the last Dickens story. Evidently the interest both in Dickens and Drood is as fresh as ever; and I have just been reading a very lively and lucid pamphlet on the subject by Mr. Aubrey Boyd, of the University of Washington. His work is particularly refreshing, in comparison with many, because he realizes that the way to detect a crime is to keep cool like the detective, and not to go mad like the criminal lunatic. Some of the interpreters of Dickens seem to have conscientiously smoked opium in the den of the Princess Puffer before offering their conclusions about Jasper. Mr. Boyd touches on some other American critics with a graceful irony. "In 1875 a certain anonymous citizen of Brattleborough, Vermont, with an assurance less typical of angels than of our countrymen, completed the book by means of a spirit pen." His own logic is sane and self-respecting, whether it establishes his own conclusion or no. Broadly, that conclusion is that the tale was meant to be not so much a tale of opium as a tale of hypnotism. As Mr. Boyd expresses it, it would have anticipated *Trilby*. He can certainly quote much in support of this in the scene of Jasper's silent domination of Rosa, and in other places. It cannot be denied that Dickens was very likely to be attracted by what was then a new scientific idea; but I hope he was not. New scientific ideas go so very stale.

Oddly enough, Mr. Boyd mentions but does not emphasize a more sensational possibility in the matter. If Jasper was a hypnotist in the rather vague romantic fashion, it seems possible that he was not the murderer at all in the material and concrete fashion. With the licence allowed to mesmerists in sensational fiction, why should not Landless have done the deed after all, but only as an automaton acting under the mesmeric eye of Jasper? This would help the theory of Mr. Boyd, who holds that Helena was to come in as a white witch or counter-hypnotist when all else failed. For all else certainly would fail, if every legal proof led nearer to the physical criminality of Landless. This is Mr. Boyd's theory and not mine; but one rather wild yet not untenable idea occurs to me in support of it. The controversy largely turns on a sentence in Forster's *Life of Dickens* about the author's intention of making a murderer describe his experience as if "some other man" had undergone it. I will mention in a moment why I think that Forster's impressions must necessarily have been often mistaken. Is it not just possible that he was mistaken here, and Dickens' meaning was something quite different which sounds somewhat the same? Is it just possible that Dickens really said: "The murderer will confess his crime, and yet when he comes to describe it, it will be the act of another man"?

The testimony of John Forster about Edwin Drood is almost always treated as if it were the sworn evidence of an expert witness on a question of fact. In reality it is merely the momentary impression, made on a sincere but not subtle mind, by the random remarks of a genius about his half-formed fancies, always confused, and in this case deliberately concealed. But, indeed, the very passage which the critics treat as exact is in itself decidedly inexact. Forster reports Dickens as announcing a new and strong idea, difficult to work and impossible to communicate for fear of spoiling the surprise. Afterwards Forster says that "the originality" was to consist of the criminal describing his crime as if it were somebody else's. Most people reading straight ahead would naturally suppose that the originality of the story was also the strong incommunicable idea of the story. They would therefore assume that Dickens, having first called the idea incommunicable, had immediately proceeded to communicate it; and hav-

ing said that his story would be spoilt by telling
his secret, had then told his secret to spoil his story.
Anyhow, it is far from clear whether Forster regarded these two ideas as identical or not. Personally, I agree with Mr. Aubrey Boyd that they were
not identical. Dickens had something in store more
striking than that trick of talking in the third person. But the fact that Forster says that it constituted the whole originality of the story is enough
to show that Forster's book is not an impreg-
nable rock of holy scripture. But, in truth, it is
absurd to treat as fixed and final, in the evidence of
Forster, ideas that were not yet fixed and final even
in the imagination of Dickens.

As to the problem of the return of Drood, I would
venture to make a distinction. I agree with Mr.
Boyd that the mere idea of Jasper "watched by the
dead" was not new enough to be incommunicable.
But it does not follow that it was not useful enough
to be used. Drood as Datchery might be an incident
in the story without being the climax of the story.
And I doubt, as Mr. Boyd does, whether Datchery
was in any case meant to be the climax of the story,
whoever he was. But while I attach little importance
to Drood being Datchery, I still think there are good
arguments for Drood being alive. The arguments
against it are all of a kind with the pedantry about
Forster; the notion of accepting most literally the

very things that are always said most lightly. Anybody might say, of an uncompleted slaying in an
unwritten story, that the man was "a murderer,"
or that he "strangled" the other man. For instance,
I think it quite fanciful of Poe to object to Mrs.
Rudge being called a "widow." A person who lives
and looks like a widow, and is legally regarded as a
widow, is called a widow. He might as well call
Dickens a liar for describing Miss Trotwood as Miss
Trotwood.

But this idea of Edwin's escape has another interest for me. I have never had a real Drood theory
of my own. But I have always had a vague notion of
my own, which nobody has ever suggested to me.
It is, if possible, even vaguer than the real notion
probably was, when Dickens first had it and Forster
first heard of it. So far as it follows anybody, it follows the admirable remark of Andrew Lang about
the very title of *The Mystery of Edwin Drood:*
"If Edwin Drood is dead, there is not much mystery
about him." By the way, is Mr. Boyd right in citing
Andrew Lang among those who accept the theory of
Helena Landless as Datchery? However, the point
is that the unfinished story is called a mystery. But
if it is only the mystery of who murdered Drood, it
is not a mystery at all. It is not even an unfinished
story at all. It is not unfinished but finished; and
there seems no need of any sequel. Multitudes of

Dickensians, including myself, have been completing a complete incident; and considerably wasting our time. As this thought is too appalling to be endured, I will throw out my own vague hint for avoiding it.

I have sometimes wondered whether the mystery of Edwin Drood may have been, not the mystery of how he was killed or escaped killing, or why he reappeared or refrained from reappearing, but something altogether different; something, for instance, in connexion with who he *was*. The mystery might date back to the last generation, to the love-affair of Grewgious, the mysterious feud of the Princess Puffer, and the apparently Asiatic past of Jasper and perhaps of Jasper's sister, the mother of Edwin Drood. In any case, I am almost certain that the story would have worked backwards as well as forwards. Otherwise I cannot see why Dickens dragged in so many things requiring retrospective explanation, such as the opium hag's hatred of Jasper. An idea occurs to me even in connexion with the pact of Edwin and Rosa: the idea of some substitution or false relationship. All this is intentionally hazy; but it has the advantage that it might make a mystery that was a mystery of Edwin Drood, and not a mystery of Dick Datchery or even of John Jasper. It would allow of his rising from the dead and even reappearing as the detective, without these things constituting the real "incommunicable" revelation. That would be, not his doing these things, but rather why he did them. If, for instance, there was some secret of his parentage or identity, he was clearly unconscious of it at the start. But Jasper's attempt might be the beginning of revelations from which he could not, or would not, disentangle himself till they were complete. This would incidentally meet the natural objection to Drood as Datchery, that though the murdered might watch the murderer, he would hardly need to detect him. Suppose he were not detecting his own death but his own birth. Suppose the real mystery began before the story. That is the floating fancy I have always had about Drood; and I am happy to say that I do not care a brass button whether there is a word of truth in it or not.

XL. ON BYRON AND TOM MOORE

I THINK there is something about Byron and his biography, and many of their comrades and contemporaries, that has not been said. This is very probably because it is not at all easy to say. I fear my own attempt to say it will sound curiously vague; and yet to my own mind it is very vivid. I feel it about Byron; I feel it about Byron's friend Moore; I even feel it about Moore's friend the Prince Regent. Byron as an individual was the least defensible of the three; but I am not going to enter here into the controversy about his private life. It will be enough to say that, upon the blackest hypothesis, the story is an excellent illustration of a truth very valuable in all confessions: that we never know the best that can be said, till we know the worst that can be said. The worst that can be said of Byron, if it was true, was not so bad as many might reasonably have supposed when it was partially hidden. It was not a sort of precocious perversion from the cradle, but a later coincidence that had the ill-luck if not the innocence of Oedipus. But putting this business altogether on one side, nobody will pretend that Byron was not a pretty aggressively bad man; and he certainly did not pretend it himself.

But it is exactly here that we have the first intellectual injustice to Byron. The very term "Byronic" has come to stand, not merely for melancholy, but for an insincere and merely melodramatic melancholy. He is represented as a swaggering and shallow fool, always parading fictitious feelings and posing as solitary only in order to attract society. Now the enemies of Byron really cannot have it both ways. They cannot accuse him of the blackest crimes, taunt him with brooding on them, and then tell him that he had nothing to brood about. They cannot accuse him, first of being a profligate, and then of being a humbug when he professed to be a profligate. His trouble cannot have been as deep as hell and as shallow as an Adelphi play. He cannot have been as black as he was painted, if he painted himself blacker than he was. And if he had been ten times blacker than anybody could possibly be, he would still have some right in reason and justice to have the case against him put intelligibly in black and white. At present the case is rather parallel to that which the stupidest sort of English people used to make against the French duel. The French duellist was called a murderer for having killed a man, and then called a coward for not having killed him. The truth was, of course, that the larger number of duels were of a normal and intermediate sort, in which men ran some sort of relative but real risk. But where there was nothing deadly there could not have been anything murderous; and where there was anything murderous there cannot have been anything unreal. So, in the poetry and pose of Byron, where there was anything guilty there must at least have been the realism of guilt.

My own reading of the riddle may be wrong, but it is extremely simple. It is that Byron was naturally a man not only of great force but of great freshness of passions; and some of these were bad passions, which he never had a reasonable religion to control. Consequently he did abominable things; as any one of us would have done if, during certain periods, he had done anything he felt inclined to do. But precisely because of his fundamental freshness, he remained young enough really to feel remorse. If he was Manfred, it proves that he was not Mephistopheles. The really dried-up diabolists do not have remorse, at least in that moral sense; a decadent Roman emperor or a Nietzschean maniac would never have poured out pessimism so warm and emotional as Byron's. There is something boyish in the sulks of Byron, precisely because he has not entirely lost the reactions into rage and sorrow which come in boyhood. Being a tolerably bad boy, and not having the heroic charity of a complete penitent, he mixed up his remorse for his own conduct with liberal cursings and vituperations of the conduct of other people. But that is exactly what anybody does do who is still young enough to be sulky. To put the point another way, there was one respect in which Byron really was not so black as he painted himself. There was one point in which he really was only a stage villain, confessing a fictitious crime. But this fiction also is one of the facts of boyhood. This insincerity also is part of the sincerity of sulks. He really was entirely wrong when he said that his heart was dead and his feelings were cold as ashes; that all freshness had gone out of him, and that nothing moved him any more.

For this tentative interpretation I will plead one small detail of defence. It does make some sort of sense of Byron's poetry, and the other views can make nothing but nonsense of it. If ever there was a gift of rhyme and rhetoric that had not lost its freshness, it was the gift of Byron. If ever there were poems, bad or good, that might have been written by an inspired boy, or possibly an intoxicated boy, they were the poems of Byron. And they are depreciated now, not at all because they are stale, but because criticism is not fresh enough to feel their freshness. Their very crudity and obviousness is part of something too simple for most modern minds to enjoy. Stevenson, in his fascinating essay on the toy theatre, has some very exact phrase about "those direct clap-trap appeals which a man is dead and buriable when he does not answer." I would not say that the excellent and sometimes exquisite critics of more recent times are dead or buriable; but I do say that their type of criticism necessarily misses the very meaning and purpose of those direct appeals. In one sense, indeed, artistic effects of the Byronic sort are not things to be criticized at all. In this case there is a real meaning in the modern substitution of the word "appreciation" for the word "criticism." These are not things that we criticize, but things which we appreciate— or do not appreciate. But those who depreciate, because they cannot appreciate, are simple people who have got hold of the wrong subject for their particular sort of appreciation.

It is illogical to argue with people who are not roused by the noise of a bugle, or by a dramatic toast suddenly proposed at a banquet, or by a blow given in public, or a voice calling on a mob to rise. And it is illogical to argue with those who never happen to have found themselves, when in a state of towering high spirits and hilarity, swinging down the road and reciting the cheerful lines, "Oh, there's not a joy the world can give like that it takes away," rising to a specially soaring gaiety with the turn of the words, "Then the mortal coldness of the soul like death itself comes down." These lines have a thousand faults, like their author, for they are alive as he was, and it was the one thing about himself that he did not know. As for their merits, an analysis of them would be entirely unsuitable to their nature. But I will mention one of the merits of the Byronic poetry in conclusion, because it is a symbol of all the rest, and that is its swiftness. Let anyone who does not know what I mean open the book and read two lyrics, the first that occur to me—the lines to Tom Moore, "My boat is on the shore and my bark is on the sea," and the verses beginning "We'll go no more a-roving." They are both very short poems, but they are much shorter than they look. They can be read, and should be read, almost in a breath, one verse leading to another as one line to another. The whole lyric goes swift and straight to its end like a single arrow; and he who appreciates it will have learned something of the nature of arrows and the nature of songs, and of why Apollo was an archer.

XLI. ON R. L. S.

I HAVE had occasion recently to read a good deal of what has recently been written about Robert Louis Stevenson. I had no need to read what was written by Robert Louis Stevenson, for I have read it all long ago and many times over; and I have remembered it, which does not seem to be the case with some who depreciate it. For I have found the critics not so much criticizing Stevenson as criticizing somebody else and putting it down to the discredit of Stevenson. The strangest things are said on the subject. One distinguished critic said that Stevenson was only an inferior imitator of Poe; which is like saying that Dickens is only one mass of plagiarism from Byron, or that *The Wallet of Kai-Lung* is a sort of reprint of Burton's *Anatomy of Melancholy*.

Stevenson was a man who came out of a world of Puritanism into a world of Pessimism. Or, rather, the point of his story was that he escaped from the first but did not enter the second. That escape was first and last an escape in pursuit of happiness, which seemed to him to be forbidden both by the religion of his ancestors and the irreligion of his contemporaries. He had to patch up a sort of makeshift philosophy of his own, which may not have been (and indeed was not) very complete or logical, but which had very vital truths in it, of a type neglected in his time. But both the truths and the errors were concerned with this problem of happiness; and not only with a thirst for happiness but with a faith in the possibility of happiness. For this reason they were not really understood then by those who sought their religion in Calvin or those who sought their philosophy in Schopenhauer. For this reason they are not likely to be understood now by people who compare him to Poe or think he only loved his hateful characters. And yet it is in connexion with this last point, and its relation to the problem of happiness, that he really might be criticized—by more penetrating critics.

The admirable essay called "The Lantern-Bearers" is an attack on realism, which might be stated thus. A realist was one who described a slum, let us say, as one monochrome grey or drab mass of factories and public-houses. And the realism was unreal; if only in the light of this single fact; that the public-houses appeared to be as grimy and greasy as the factories. Whereas, of course, to the people using them there was exactly the same difference that a clerk feels between a late night's work at the office and a pleasant theatre-supper in a restaurant. It is silly to set out to describe the chiaroscuro of a slum and then to call yourself an artist because you are blind to the difference between light and shade. Somewhat in the same spirit Stevenson set himself to pointing out that the amount of pleasure most people got out of life could not be measured, at any rate, in terms of this treatmeant of externals; because the externals were unattractive, even in the case of things with a notorious power of attraction. If we want to know why Stevenson liked Skelt's Juvenile Drama we cannot discover it by sending a sheet of Penny Plain and Twopence Coloured to be entered for an examination at the Academy School; if we want to know why the slum-dweller likes the public-house, we cannot know by sending a refined West End critic on a weekly paper to look at it. The principle applies, of course, to many who would be equally disinclined to look at the public-house. A milder sort of realist delighted in describing the dreary life of some spinster in the suburbs, who did nothing but paint in water-colours or wash up the tea-things. And here again it missed the whole point: that she painted in water-colours for pleasure; whereas nobody ever washed up tea-things for pleasure. How much pleasure she got out of it is known only to God and not to realistic novelists; but it is bad psychology to wash away the water-colours in the common element of water, while entirely ignoring the element of colour. A principle of this sort is applied in "The Lantern-Bearers" to a variety of types of men; and even to the type of the miser. Men are represented as generally a race of unreasonably happy ostriches; each man with his head in a hobby, as in a hole in the ground. The view needs correction by complementary truths; but so far as it goes it is unquestionably true. In the science of psychology even illusions are facts; just as even dreams are data. And it is true in this sense that every man knows what he wants and in that degree knows it to be worth wanting. No man was ever in love with a slut, but only with somebody whom others perceived to be a slut. And it is not even true to say that a man gets drunk in sordid surroundings, since it is the very definition of his drunkenness that they cease to be sordid. I am not here considering the proper limits of this argument, as in the case of the drunkard or the miser. I merely remark that when the realists held up before Stevenson Degas's picture of the two grey-faced dipsomaniacs sitting over their dull green drink and said, "This is the picture of Absinthe," it was his immediate impulse to answer, "That is not even a picture of Absinthe; for men only drink absinthe that things may not look like that."

Fortunately, however, he did not recommend taking refuge in absinthe: he recommended taking refuge in Skeltery. He denied that the heroine of the Penny Plain and Twopence Coloured could never be coloured merely because superficial observers thought her rather plain. He did, in his most characteristic works, set out forthwith to fill up the too plain outlines of the old juvenile melodrama with the colours of carefully selected and discriminating art; he sought to bring out what had really been so intensely delightful in those obscure delights; and to interpret them anew to grown-up people, without losing the memory that had made them peculiarly precious to children. It is this psychological experiment—the attempt to find out whether the fantastic pleasure of infancy *could* be continued through the maturer development of manhood—that is the special interest of Stevenson. Anybody who does not understand that this *was* the nature of his experiment knows nothing about the matter or the man, and is really criticizing somebody else.

Nevertheless, it is odd that those who seem to have something very like a spite against Stevenson should not have noted the real dangers or difficulties raised by his psychological argument; which is sound enough as far as it goes; but might be made to go a great deal too far. Though thoroughly healthy in motive, it is much too subjective to be quite healthy in method. It might indeed be used to justify the miser or even the murderer; and, in real life, Stevenson might well have had more sympathy with the murderer than the miser. Exactly what it lacked was something which Stevenson subconsciously sought but never found: a religion in the sense of a rule; a real trust in some external standard as a reality. Without that, a sympathy with the child's joy in beholding the dragon may eventually turn into a sympathy with the dragon's joy in eating the child. What is needed is the recognition that there are joys that lead to the highest joy and joys that lead to the lowest despair. For want of a recognition of this, the Stevensonian philosophy might have been counted wanting; though, in fact, Stevenson understood it better than superficial readers might suppose. Yet these critics are such very superficial readers that they have not noted even this superficial example. They have merely called him selfish and not seen that he was objective; even when he was unselfishly subjective; even when he was subjective for others. But the critics do not blame him for his real defect: that he had not the clear and ultimate idea of truth. The explanation is probably simple: that they have not got it themselves.

Between Stevenson and Poe I confess I can hardly imagine a stranger or more puzzling parallel. I leave aside, in deference to such æsthetic critics, everything except æsthetic criticism. I say nothing of secondary matters like morality and philosophy and a whole outlook on life. I toss aside such trifles as belief, doubt, despair, pessimism, piety, faith, hope, and charity. Considering art simply as a method of calling up certain visions or adumbrating certain atmospheres, it seems to me that no two great artists could possibly be more unlike each other than Stevenson and Poe. The atmospheres they tried to create were quite opposite; the technical tricks by which they tried to create them were quite opposite. It was the purpose of Poe to suggest not merely horror but hopelessness. It was the whole point of Stevenson that he never did suggest hopelessness even when he suggested horror. Or, to put the matter another way, he always suggested a fight, even when it was a hopeless fight. The two brothers of the house of Durrisdeer go down fighting to the last. The people of the house of Usher never begin fighting even from the first. I find it difficult to believe, even in face of the text, that Dr. Jekyll and Mr. Hyde will not go on fighting, if it were only fighting in hell. But when the other gentleman had his rather one-sided conversation with the raven, that raven did not croak over a battlefield.

As I have said, I did not mean merely the matter of moral atmosphere, but of purely artistic atmosphere. Stevenson's technical method is lean, wiry, taut, and alert. If he seems too much to be picking his words, to be watchful of his style, it is because he is above all things very wide-awake. It is the whole point and pleasure and beauty of the poetry of Poe

that he is half asleep. Consider those dreamy melo-
dies, those drowsy repetitions, like everlasting echoes
of an endless snore. And compare them with the
short-lined, sharply worded verses of "R. L. S.,"
generally rather too bald and angular to be quite
good poetry. Poe was above all things luxuriant.
He loved, in the literal sense of the phrase, the
luxury of woe. He was at home on rich but sombre
cushions "that the lamp-light gloated o'er"; but
it was not only the lamp-light that gloated. I defy
anyone to find one sentence in all the collected works
of Robert Louis Stevenson in which it can be said
that he gloated. It might be said that he sometimes
tasted too fastidiously or that he sometimes snapped
up too sharply. But he never wallowed in purple
seas of woe; and it was the whole point of Stevenson
that the seas were infinite and unfathomable. Poe's
people are not people who have been made unhappy,
like Henry Durie or Robert Herrick, or who have
made themselves unhappy, like Dr. Jekyll or Mark-
heim; they are people who never could conceivably
have been happy. They are unhappy before they are
unfortunate. They are tragic before their tragedy begins. With Poe the mood was the fundamental thing;
and it was a mood of incurable melancholy. It was,
of course, the essence of the Stevensonian spirit that
the melancholy was not incurable even if the misfor-
tune was incurable.

But I am not speaking for the moment of such ethical motives, but merely of artistic methods and artistic effects. And this vigilance and alertness and spirit of choice is in the very style of Stevenson. It is also in the very imagery of Stevenson. He loved above all things what was clean-cut and clearly coloured; nothing could be less like the magnificent monochrome of the other writer's dark libraries and dim corridors. The things that Stevenson liked were things like the chip of hard wood hacked out of the wooden sign of the Admiral Ben Bow by the cutlass of Billy Bones the buccaneer. They were things like the crutch of the horrible cripple, that went flashing in the tropical sun sped on its errand of death. In short, the things he loved were almost always solid and were generally self-evident in the sun. Even when they were not, as in the duel scene of *The Master of Ballantrae*, the starlight seems as hard as the steel and the candle-flames as steady as the swords. Surely nothing could have so little of the dark halls and drowsy odours in which the brain of the other heroes brilliantly decayed. Stevenson afterwards regretted the exaggeration which had made Mrs. Durie wipe the sword-blade by driving it into the frozen soil. But it was a truly Stevensonian exaggeration, for it was an exaggeration of what was hard and acute. He was always working with a sharp blade on a hard ground.

This fact appears in his real failure as well as his real success. Where he failed, as compared with the great Victorian novelists, was in being too severe with himself and with his characters. He described a character in a few strokes where the Victorians described him in a hundred little touches. The strokes were artistically exactly right—almost too right. For while the few strokes only give the impression of being right, the many touches give the impression of being real. Long John Silver's crutch always comes in at the right moment, and is almost too solid to be true. The Colonel's bamboo cane comes in quite casually in Thackeray's novel, and we cannot remember how many times it has been mentioned; but we are all the more sure that there really was a cane and that there really was a Colonel. There is no gossip about Stevenson's characters as there is about Thackeray's characters. There is no over-flowing of trivial things, or, better still, of irrelevant things. There is no halo of hearsay or indirect impressions. Stevenson was relentlessly relevant; he limited himself to words so perfect and so few that his figures were really too clear to be convincing. He knew this well himself, being an admirable critic.

On the moral side the meaning of his position seems also to be entirely missed. Yet it is symbolized in the same imagery of sunbeams and sword-blades. Death in Stevenson is brighter than life in Poe. And

the point of his position in history is that he came at
the precise moment when he could resist a pessimistic
spirit, even in accepting parts of a pessimistic philosophy. Living in that Victorian phase, he accepted
the struggle for life as described in terms of natural
selection; but declared himself ready to enjoy the
struggle like a struggle of pirates and picturesque
sailors. When opinion was passing through its most
depressing phase, Stevenson, like the men who did
not differ except in opinions, refused altogether to
despair except in opinion. He resolved to keep the
mood militant and sanguine whatever the theories
might be. That fine essay, *"Pulvis et Umbra,"* which
was so much misunderstood, was truly the defiance of
an optimistic man to a pessimistic world, even if it
were a pessimistic universe. I am the last person alive
to think it a true and complete view of the universe.
But, in order to appreciate it, one must appreciate the
period through which the world was passing—the
decadent darkness of the 'nineties. I for one remember it very well, for it surrounded my boyhood and
early youth, and my first literary impulse was to fight
against it. But there are many of my own age to
testify with me that they would hardly have been
able to fight against it, or even live through it, but
for the spirit and the genius of Robert Louis Stevenson.

XLII. ON THOMAS HARDY.

THOMAS HARDY, the maker of great tragedies, had through all his life learned the noblest lesson of the grand Greek tragedies of whose high thunders his voice was perhaps the last reverberation. He may be called a heathen rather than a heretic; for he was never near enough to Christianity to contradict it. But in none of his contradictions, such as they were, was there anything of that special sort of insolence against which the Greek tragedy warned heroes and kings. He was often provocative; but he was never proud. Down to the last days when he received a universal veneration as the greatest of living Englishmen, he retained a splendidly unconscious simplicity. An editor of a magazine told me that Hardy sent in his poems almost timidly, like a beginner, apologizing for crudity, even offering to correct mistakes. Even without the great work, that would convey something of the atmosphere of a great man.

The valuable word "atmosphere" has been somewhat vulgarized and overworked like other words of the kind. In criticism, for some time past, we have rather lived in an atmosphere of atmospheres. It might be correct to call the Celtic Twilight an atmosphere; for in the particular mood in which "love is less kind than the grey twilight" it is natural that even the figure of the lover or the lady should be a shadow even mistier than the mist. It is natural to speak of the rich narcotic atmosphere of certain passages of Poe or De Quincey. But the phrase does some injustice to work in which the air is clear enough to be ignored. It does some injustice to scenes in which the objects are solid enough to be seen and even handled. There is a sort of description that gives us something much more positive and satisfying than a concert of strange smells in a dark room. And when literary critics say that the tales of Thomas Hardy are full of the "atmosphere" of Dorsetshire or of Wessex, they do some injustice to what is really powerful in his prose. He had in fact a great love of shapes that are not shadows. He can make a picture which is something more than a picture; because it is not flat. It is like a picture full of coloured statues, and has the depth of a stage. There is something symbolic of him in that minor episode in *Tess*, when the rascal returns as a revivalist, and paints all along the wide fence across the country-side the large and flaming letters of his gospel. Hardy's gospel could hardly be mistaken for good news. But he painted it in much the same large open-air alphabet; generally as picturesque but always as plain. His novels and poems are full of a sort of solid antics that stick to the memory almost apart from the meaning. They might be called the practical jokes of a pessimist. A very typical example is the poem about the prodigal who, returning home, thinks he sees his father the huntsman afar off, conspicuous by his red coat; when his father has long been dead and a red coat is hung on a scarecrow. That, of course, is very characteristic of Hardy in every aspect: the view of life which is something more than tragic irony and approaches sometimes to a sort of torturers' mockery. But though the dark story is very dark, the red coat is still very bright. The actual technical method is at once lively and materialistic; and it is a little misleading to talk of it as atmosphere. The point is rather in that very vividness and objectivity with which the vermilion coat glows across the empty air. In that little tragedy there is a mistake, but nothing so merciful as a mist.

Hardy has not only given us, as is so often said, the air of the West Country; it is but just to say that he has given us the earth, the common clay, the stones and certainly the thorns and weeds. But there is another sense in which we may accept and even carry further the judgment of those who talk of the atmosphere of Hardy's Wessex. There was in one sense a special atmosphere, a spiritual atmosphere, though it was probably not so much the atmosphere of Wessex as the atmosphere of Hardy. And about that it is much more difficult to speak impartially, since it is impossible to speak impersonally. We have in Hardy a man of great sincerity and not a little simplicity; such a man could not but work from deep if not always conscious convictions; and anybody equally rooted in the opposite convictions will find it difficult to write of him without controversy. He was not a neutral or a non-combatant, and can never have wished to be treated as one. I will not pretend to sympathize with his philosophy as a truth; but I think it is quite possible to sympathize with it as an error; or, in other words, to understand how the error arose.

What we call the pessimism of Thomas Hardy had two roots. Both, I think, were rather historical than personal; in other words, I doubt whether he himself knew where they came from. The first cause was the neglect and decay of English agriculture. Anybody living in the ancient and beautiful English counties, during the last century or so, was living in a dying civilization. He was like a man hopelessly loving and inevitably losing the last traditions of the Old South in America, which had so many better things along with its aristocracy and its slavery. We also in England have an Old South. That also ran too much to aristocrats and not a little to slaves. But that also has been left to slide into poverty and decay, while the great industrial towns drank the life-blood of the land. And among the hundred signs of that historic oblivion or betrayal this is one: the pessimism of the poets. The Songs of the Shropshire Lad have the same dreary tang as those others that were the Songs of a Dorset Lad. Housman is a better poet than Hardy, simply considered as a poet; some may say because he is more of a scholar and less of a rustic. But whichever is the greater poet, it would be hard to say which was the greater pessimist. Both could doubtless give reasons for the unfaith that was in them; but I doubt whether the reasons would be the causes. And I suspect that one of the causes was in the general social aimlessness of the deserted country-side; of men that had lost the shrine of the peasant and never found the forum of the citizen. They had neither private property as a peasant understands it nor public property as a citizen understands it; they were the servants of the rich—when the rich were growing poor.

The other root of the philosophy would need an exposition merely philosophical—not to say theological. It was the final effect of the strange interlude of Calvinism. It will be noted that Hardy's pessimism was never really agnosticism. It was not even atheism. It was a strange sort of demoniac monism, which conceived a cosmic centre immediately responsible for the most minute and remote results of everything, and which he was always angrily reproaching with its responsibility. This was the inevitable ultimate effect of that total disappearance of the noble conception of Free Will, that had been the most Christian thing in all Christian theology. The Puritans abolished the larger liberty of the soul in fighting for the smaller liberty of the sect or the printing-press or the vote. Thus it came natural to Hardy to think, in a truly Calvinistic style, that the deity must have predestined Tess to damnation, instead of damning the people who treated her badly; and it could not be long before such a deity was treated as a devil. Between these two things—the subconscious sorrow of the dying fields and the old heathen sense of doom, that had returned to England in the Puritan form of damnation—Hardy grew up as the heir of tragedy. It is well that even that history and that heresy produced one great man before they perished.

It must also be remembered that it was long ago and during a pessimistic fashion that he labelled himself a pessimist. There is much to show that he mellowed in later life and grew acquainted with more gracious moods. His own personality was always in the best sense gracious, being full not only of humanity but humility. Bitterly as he had quarrelled with a demon who did not exist—a demon whom he did not even believe to exist—he never quarrelled with the human beings who do exist, and are therefore so much more aggravating. And he seems himself to have come to doubt whether he had not wasted on the former quarrel a fire that should have been given entirely to the latter sympathy:

> " 'You have not said what you meant to say,'
>   Said my own voice speaking to me:
> 'That the greatest of things is charity.' "

Certainly there is no greater thing to say, and he often said it greatly. But his provincial traditions hid from him a larger meaning of the word, in the mouths of the older mystics who spoke of charity towards God.

THE END

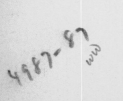